Reagan and Reality

Reagan and Reality

The Two Californias

EDMUND G. (PAT) BROWN

PRAEGER PUBLISHERS
New York • Washington • London

PRAEGER PUBLISHERS
111 Fourth Avenue, New York, N.Y. 10003, U.S.A.
5, Cromwell Place, London S.W.7, England
Published in the United States of America in 1970
by Praeger Publishers, Inc.
© 1970 by Praeger Publishers, Inc.
All rights reserved
Library of Congress Catalog Card Number: 71–108752
Printed in the United States of America

To the thirty-one Governors
of California who preceded me—and to those
who will follow Ronald Reagan

Contents

Preface

I love this beautiful and exciting state of California, and I believe in the nobility and worth of democratic government. That is why I am writing this book—because I feel that both are threatened today.

The threat is represented and led by Ronald Reagan.

This book is about his record as Governor, how it fits into the contemporary pattern of politics in the state, and what it could mean to the rest of the nation.

There are two states of California today, and they are in conflict. The split is not just a polarization toward radical political attitudes, and I am referring not only to the differences between northern and southern California, which *are* profound. The most dangerous and significant conflict today is between the realities of the California society and the illusions of the Reagan Governorship. The real state of California is complex, diverse, and changing, and it imposes difficult demands on its people. Reagan's state—his perception of the California society—is simple, rigid, and unchanging, and his influence as Governor is lulling the people into acceptance of his comforting, simplistic images. The simple state of Ronald Reagan and the complex state of California, I believe, are on a collision course.

This is not an "objective" book. My viewpoint on the subject could not possibly be objective: Reagan defeated me for re-election, after I had served two terms as Governor; he set out to reverse much of what I had worked to build in California; and his performance has confirmed my initial distaste for the man as a radical politician.

Though obviously "unobjective" and strongly critical, I have endeavored to be accurate and responsible in my analysis and narrative of Reagan's record. The facts, quotations, and details were carefully researched and checked.

If any reader wants other viewpoints on Reagan, they are available in book form. Highly favorable accounts of his life and record have been published, and a few neutral, "objective" books on him are still in print. It has not been my job in this book to review or defend my administration; I have included brief accounts of my policies and programs primarily as a means of comparison to clarify Reagan's radical departures from the past.

This book is not and cannot be definitive, and it is by no means a biography of Reagan. The details of his personal life have been covered thoroughly in many lengthy, printed narratives. Some aspects of his performance as Governor have been treated only briefly here. I have qualified some judgments and conclusions because many of the conflicts and controversies in which Reagan is involved remain unresolved, and the story of his failures, successes, and battles continues.

Publication of this book coincides with a gubernatorial campaign in California, in which Reagan is seeking re-election. I hope it will be useful to many voters who wish to learn from a more critical, in-depth account of his Governorship than the news media and magazines have been able to offer. But this book is not intended to stand as a campaign weapon. I have consciously refrained from promoting my own political party or its candidates in the 1970 election, to avoid any excessive partisanship and to avoid dating the material—much of which I believe will be interesting and significant for a long time after the 1970 elections. Interest in this book is also justified beyond the limited region of California. Reagan has been described as a political phenomenon of national potential; my book seeks to clear up some of the mystery of his sudden rise to power and prominence, and frequently places his political significance in a national framework.

I offer one final disclaimer. My interest in and concern for California politics and government is as strong as during any time of my professional involvement. But my days as a candidate are over; there is no selfish, ulterior political purpose to this book. And to modify any possible impression that I am a solitary Reagan critic engaged in a lonely effort for vindication, I have quoted extensively from other responsible critics of the Governor, including some of the state's Republican-oriented newspapers. There are also extensive excerpts from Reagan's press conferences and other of his public statements. They are included in order to offer something of the unique flavor of the man's words and attitudes and because many of his statements are so self-incriminating that they provide more graphic testimony to his failures than any outside criticism.

I tapped many sources of information for the material in this book, and interviewed many perceptive and knowledgeable individuals of different viewpoints, and am grateful to all of them for their help. My special thanks go to Win Griffith, who gave great assistance to this effort.

As a man and a politician, I have always preferred to be positive, and hope that, if I am remembered as Governor, the salient impression will be that of a constructive leader and builder for California. That is the personal reason why this has not been a pleasant project—writing a basically negative book. But it is, I believe, a *necessary* book, and one that I hope will stimulate more positive involvement by people in the beleaguered democratic political process of today.

Los Angeles, California
April, 1970

Reagan and Reality

1

A State of Diversity

A few minutes after midnight, on January 2, 1967, Ronald Reagan was sworn in as California's thirty-third Governor. During the inaugural ceremonies in the rotunda of the State Capitol, the new Governor turned to U.S. Senator George Murphy—also a former actor—and quipped, "Well, George, here we are back on the late show."

As Reagan's predecessor, I watched the inaugural ceremony with a full appreciation of its seriousness and importance. I was in Palm Springs, viewing the impressive scenes on television, trying to forget the sting of my defeat by Reagan, and groping for some sense of reality to Reagan's performance.

It wasn't easy. The period between the November election and the end of my second term in January was a difficult time of adjustment for me. A few days before, I had written in my diary: "I start a new career at 61. Neither Bernice [my wife] nor I are very happy."

Despite a slight feeling of relief that the burdens of the Governorship were off my back and despite my instinct to wish Reagan well, I couldn't help feeling an element of unreality about the inaugural scene in Sacramento—and an anxious concern for California.

Reagan had not explained—nor has he ever explained—the mystery of his choice to be sworn in as Governor in the middle of the night.

Some of his assistants hinted that the reason was to prevent any last-minute appointments or binding decisions by me, a strange and unfounded suspicion, because there was no legal possibility for such last-minute actions.

Some of Reagan's friends speculated that he, an old fan of astrological forecasts, had chosen the midnight hour as a propitious time on the basis of the positions of the stars.

Neither explanation was ever confirmed. The midnight inauguration remained a strange and mysterious break from tradition.

But more than Reagan's quip about the "late show," more than the odd timing of the ceremony, a key remark in his inaugural address struck me as unreal.

"For many years now," he said, "you and I have been shushed like children and told there are no simple answers to the complex problems which are beyond our comprehension. Well, the truth is, there *are* simple answers. . . ."

That comment jolted me back to an awareness of the extraordinarily complex realities of the California society, in contrast to the unreal illusions and simple images of the ceremony in Sacramento.

A few days before, after vacating the Governor's office and mansion in Sacramento, I had thought once again about those realities as I flew south for a rest in Palm Springs. I always valued the experience of flying over California. It was a chance not just to get away from the ever ringing telephone and the exhausting demands of the Governorship. I even

liked the relatively slow speed and low altitude of the pro-
peller-driven airplanes provided during my Governorship.
On flights over the state, I usually ignored the jammed briefcase at my side and kept my face glued to the window, so I
could watch the immense variety of California. Often, on my
request, the pilot would vary the route, to let me view the
Mother Lode country in the golden foothills of the Sierras of
the fog-framed Coastal Mountain Range. In the air, I was
able to pull my mind away from the intricate and urgent
details of individual state problems. For a few hours in an
airplane, I could regain a clear view of the total reality of
the state, of the wholeness of the California land and
society.

When you fly over the full length of California, all the
clichés fade away. Lulled by the distant and detached perspective in space, you begin to reject the rigid and often negative generalizations about this state. California does not seem
rootlessly ready to slide into the sea, or on the verge of disintegration from the confusions and conflicts of its 20 million
people, or about to be blotted out by an apron of asphalt.
For more than a thousand miles, you see extraordinary
beauty, unspoiled open lands, and soil rich with the colors of
life and productivity. The cities, when they can be seen
through the smog, seem serene, symmetrical, and orderly.

Even Governors, for all their blustery confidence, can be
reduced to silent wonder at the one quality and cliché about
California that cannot be exaggerated: its diversity. Viewed
from the air, the differences of the changing landscape are
infinite. From moment to moment and mile to mile, California becomes moist forest or gray desert, jagged mountains
or graceful hills, vast and flat farmlands or great quilted
vistas of cities and suburbs.

Down on the ground after the lofty reflection, one finds the
same awesome diversity in the realities of California's society
and politics. The state is too diverse to be defined precisely

and briefly. It is absurd for national reporters to seek simple, blanket summaries of California after spending three days in Los Angeles (it takes that much time for a driving tour of the place), three days in San Francisco (reporters like its night life), and one day in Sacramento (its night life is nil). I have lived in California all my life, served for eight years as State Attorney General, worked for eight years as Governor, and wondered often about its true identity—and am more reluctant than ever to generalize about the state. But the reporters and the sociologists keep coming for their seven-day, "in-depth" surveys. The most honest of them usually go back to write stream-of-consciousness accounts consisting of appropriately isolated impressions or admit meekly that California *is* the set of clichés that others had called it, but also much more—too much, in fact, to figure out.

As Governor, I tried to steer national reporters away from the easy generalizations and to make them face the broader truth behind such clichés as these:

California is two states, north and south. Legally, the land between the Mexican and Oregon borders is one state, but the societies of people separated by the Tehachapi Mountains are as different as night and day. Northern Californians, particularly in the San Francisco area, tend to be politically progressive, tolerant of divergent viewpoints, and significantly influenced by intellectual leaders. Southern Californians, particularly in such booming areas as Orange County, tend to be politically reactionary, intolerant of individual deviations from majority WASP attitudes, and suspicious of intellectuals. I like both parts of the state, but I sympathize with northern Californians who worry—with justification—about the increasing political dominance of the south. (I admit to personal prejudice on the grounds that I always won a higher proportion of votes in the north—and huge majorities in San Francisco, where the people knew me best.) The

difference in attitudes and needs of northern Californians
and southern Californians is profound and creates bitter
rivalries and conflicts. In the mid-1960's, I was inclined to
support a bill in the legislature to split California into two,
legal states, and would have pushed it except for a pending
state water project, which required conciliation between
north and south.

California's growth is extraordinary. The rate of the state's
population growth has declined a bit in recent years, but the
phenomenal growth continues. The population has approximately doubled during every twenty-year period of its history, including the most recent two decades, when it soared
from 10 million to 20 million. When I became Governor in
1959, nothing impressed me more than the prospect of the
state's continuing growth, and the necessity to invest in the
future to avoid chaos or a diminished quality of life. To me,
the state's growth was a fact that the government had to recognize, prepare for, and try to channel constructively.

California is the "wave of the future." Who knows? It is
true that many national social patterns first emerged in California, and some aspects of the life style of Californians do
influence the tastes and aspirations of other Americans. But
it is shaky business to peer into the future on any grounds,
particularly on the changing and unpredictable grounds of
California society. California may or may not portend the
face and features of the larger American society, but it is
clearly and often *first* in exhibiting some new national taste
or attitude, either positive or negative. The state has re-
corded impressive "firsts" in the methods and quality of its
higher education system; it also produced, in Berkeley, the
first incidence of the major campus riots that have swept the
country.

Californians are "hedonistic." Of course most Californians
pursue pleasure. If they do so in greater numbers than in

other areas of the country, the explanation is simple: Blessed with good climate and affluence, Californians have abundant opportunity for fun. But the notion that Californians are consumed by a corrupting orgy of self-gratification is nonsense. Californians work, worry, serve, give, and strive toward noble goals as much as Americans anywhere.

California is a "rootless, restless nonculture." The favorite cliché, perhaps, of the national reporter is that California lacks a distinct culture of its own. Of course, California has a culture, and not just in terms of its fine artistic institutions. The California culture simply hasn't had the time or the stagnant social environment to become fixed in a mold of single architectural, musical, and life styles. The California culture defies narrow description; its features are diffuse and its essential characteristics are *diversity* and change.

The element of change in California politics, the unpredictable quality that so often confuses national reporters, is starkly dramatic in a comparison of the 1962 and 1966 gubernatorial elections. In 1962, I decisively defeated Richard Nixon for the Governorship. Four years later, Ronald Reagan clobbered me for the Governorship.

Why?

No single factor, no one issue ever decides the result of an election campaign. There are many causes—some of them clear and easily identified, others obscure or subtle—that finally give one man victory and another defeat in a free election in a large state. But there are some specific elements in the 1962 and 1966 elections that are fascinating to consider and compare.

Despite his narrow loss in the Presidential election in 1960 to John F. Kennedy, Nixon was an imposing political figure in California as the 1962 election campaign approached. To many Democrats, including some of my advisers, he was downright intimidating as a prospective opponent. He was a native Californian and had never lost an election in the state. He had served as Vice President of the United States for eight years and still enjoyed some of the political magic of his long and close association with Dwight D. Eisenhower. In 1960, he won in California over Kennedy, and the national results of that election were close enough to give him respectability for his effort.

My advisers and I also recognized Nixon as an intelligent, though not brilliant, man, and a shrewd, tough, and occasionally demagogic campaigner. We were proud of the record of my first term as Governor, but we were frankly scared of the Nixon threat to my re-election—particularly when the reliable opinion polls in early 1962 revealed that he was far ahead of me in the favor of California voters.

Politicians, particularly of my generation, like to think that they can control events, influence millions, and shape history by their own efforts. The attitude is, perhaps, a comforting bit of self-delusion, but it also helps give the candidate a tough kernel of confidence when he is identified as an underdog in a campaign. In early 1962, I refused to become fatalistic about my own chances for re-election or awed by the apparent political stature and popularity of Nixon in California.

A major factor in the 1962 election, I am convinced, was strictly personal: I set out to renew my confidence and energies after realizing that three years in the demanding duties of the Governorship had to some extent tired me and insulated me from my own strongest qualities as a man and politician. It was perhaps an unorthodox preliminary preparation for a major election campaign, but I simply broke away from the habitual routine of my life and attitudes to recharge my batteries—physically, spiritually, and mentally.

First, I took off thirty pounds in a period of about forty days, going from 210 down to 180. I stuck to a protein diet,

cut out all cocktails and each morning my wife and I rose at
5:00 A.M. to play a fast eighteen holes of golf on a course outside Sacramento—with no caddies, no carts. The result was
that I felt fit and vigorous physically—a significant asset for
a politician facing a long and arduous campaign.

Second, I sought spiritual renewal by spending three days
at a Jesuit retreat house in the lovely hills near Los Gatos.
For three days, I was silent, not saying a word, giving myself
the chance and the peace for prayer and spiritual awareness.
The retreat was enhanced by the priest who led it, Fr. James
Toner, a stimulating, enthusiastic, faithful man. At the end
of my stay, I felt deeply strengthened spiritually.

Third, I broke away from the exhausting hourly demands
of the Governor's office to seek mental and intellectual renewal. My staff and I spent a full week at a friend's home in
the southern California desert to review everything we had
done in the Governorship, everything that still needed to be
done for California, all the facts, issues, and problems of the
state's political and social realities. By the end of that week,
I felt that I had a coherent understanding of the state of
California and that the details of its needs were at my finger-
tips.

Sophisticated political analysts might consider that three-
phased preparation for the 1962 campaign corny. But the
physical, spiritual, and mental renewal made me fully ready
and *confident,* as the campaign began. I shrugged at the
negative results of the political opinion polls, took a detached
look at Richard Nixon and felt that I was the better man.
An attitude of genuine confidence within a candidate has a
way of conveying itself to the people; it becomes a powerful
factor in a campaign.

In 1962, Nixon seemed hesitant, unsure, tired, and ner-
vous. Instead of cultivating additional respect for his years
near the pinnacle of national power, he often came across as

condescending in this campaign for state office. He thought he knew and understood California and its issues, but he didn't. He had been away from the state and not really involved intimately in its issues since his campaign for the Senate in 1950. And I suspect that Nixon simply lacked that inner confidence, which I have described earlier; he seemed uncertain about his positions on many issues, and I doubt that he felt well physically.

Nixon was well financed in 1962, and his basic campaign speech was carefully and effectively contrived for its political effect. Technically, however, his campaign was lacking, particularly in its use of television. He had not yet found that combination of masterful coaching and personal manner which was an essential part of his Presidential campaign of 1968. It has occurred to me that if Nixon had been as well coached for TV in 1962 as in 1968, he might have beaten me for the Governorship.

The former Vice President was also hurt by some specific issues and developments in his bid for the California Governorship. He had a tough Republican primary fight with conservative Joseph C. Shell, and the wounds of that battle did not heal between June and November. Columnist Drew Pearson revealed at a key point in the campaign that Nixon, as Vice President, had borrowed $325,000 from Howard Hughes—a highly questionable step for a man in high public office and a new issue, which put Nixon on the defensive through the critical months of the campaign. In October, the Cuban missile crisis frightened the American people; Californians, as much as any group, tended to rally behind President Kennedy in the emergency. I suspended all formal campaigning during the crisis, flew to Washington to confer with the President, and worked there with other Governors (including Nelson Rockefeller of New York) and military officials on a Civil Defense committee. Nixon seemed out of it and self-serving, as he continued his tours of shopping centers and local television studios.

Generally, the people of California were in a positive, progressive, and forward-looking mood in 1962. They knew that their state would soon become the Number One State in the Nation, and they identified with the efforts of government, both in Washington and Sacramento, to plan and pay for a better future. It was a good and optimistic time for America. The people wanted leaders with ideals, plans, proposals, programs. Richard Nixon, whose political philosophy is negative rather than progressive, was out of tune with the time and the temper of the people in 1962.

(It is with some amusement now that I recall the near unanimous view that Nixon was finished in politics after the 1962 election. His million-vote defeat was devastating enough, everyone said. His own truculent "You won't have Nixon to shaft anymore" statement on election night was a self-inflicted *coup de grace,* all believed. How strange politics is; now Nixon is President.)

In the mid-1960's, the temper of the people was transformed. In my second term as Governor of California, I endeavored to refine the programs and efforts begun in my first term. The foundations, I felt, had been laid for California to build toward the growth of the state. In my second term, the prime purpose was to improve the *quality* of state programs and not just keep ahead of the great *quantity* of needs for state services. But, by 1966, California's political attitudes seemed to sour, or, at least, the people grew terribly confused by events that seemed beyond their comprehension and beyond the control of their leaders.

John F. Kennedy was assassinated in 1963.

Berkeley exploded in student turmoil and protest in 1964.

Watts burst into flames, bloody violence, and racial fury in 1965.

And then came Reagan.

Ronald Reagan's 1966 victory over me for the Governorship was no fluke of politics nor was it merely the result of a periodic swing of the political pendulum from left to right. The majority of Californians were ripe for a radically different type of Governor and immensely receptive to the personality, style, and philosophy of Reagan. I doubt that any efforts of mine to renew myself physically, spiritually, and mentally could have changed the results of the 1966 election.

In contrast to my initial respect for Nixon as a formidable opponent, I greatly underestimated Reagan as the campaign approached. Some of my advisers and many leading California Democrats blithely dismissed him, with ridicule, as a prospective pushover.

We had our neat, logical reasons for thinking that Reagan would be easy to beat:

• He was a fading, aging actor who had never really gone very far beyond roles in grade-B movies and whose most recent prominence was as the host for the mediocre *Death Valley Days* TV series.

• He had never run for nor been appointed to any public office and was completely inexperienced in the field of government.

• In his adult life, he had flip-flopped from enthusiastic advocacy of ultraliberal Democratic causes and candidates to a firm and fond embracing of far–right-wing Republican celebrities and attitudes.

• His only recent political exposure had been his unqualified and widely televised support for the 1964 Republican Presidential Candidate, Barry Goldwater, who was trounced in California as well as nationally.

Ronald Reagan for Governor of California? We thought the notion was absurd and rubbed our hands in gleeful anticipation of beating this politically inexperienced, right-wing extremist and aging actor in 1966.

One of Reagan's huge advantages was that he was not identified by the public as a politician. While I emphasized my many years of experience in politics and government, Reagan emphasized what he called the "citizen-politician" approach to government, a clever euphemism for a non-politician. I relied inevitably on the liberal logic that the people wanted a Governor who was politically skilled and qualified for governmental leadership. Reagan sensed that there was a new surge of disdain for politicians in the land and uninhibitedly proclaimed his contempt for politicians and politics. "Let's take politics out of government," he said again and again. My reaction was that such a move would be about as difficult as taking the flour out of bread, but the majority of Californians were receptive to Reagan's anti-politics stance.

Traditionally, Americans tend to be suspicious of politicians and government. That element of mistrust may remain submerged for a while, if things are going well in society, taxes are not biting too deeply, and political leaders convey that subtle, appealing quality described variously as charisma, style, or class. But if the people are uneasy or angry about the tide of social events, taxes are hitting them hard and personally, and their leaders are boring, the anti-politics instinct surges to the surface, and the "rascals" are thrown out.

In 1966, Reagan profited on all three counts. Californians were angry about the student demonstrations and violence at Berkeley and indignant about the portion of their taxes going to pay for the education of "those damned kids." Fear was rampant among white citizens after the ghetto riots in Watts in 1965 and later in the Hunter's Point district of San Francisco; the people tended to equate Negro unrest with *all* crime, which was rising sharply, and to turn all the more against welfare and antipoverty costs. And, to be frank, a majority of Californians were simply bored with me, the other Democratic state officers, and the Democratic Party in general. We had been in power for seven years; our faces and voices were familiar to the point of dullness, if not contempt. Californians, perhaps more conditioned than most Americans to want and expect new things and faces frequently, just couldn't get inspired by what some called "that tired old crowd in Sacramento."

Reagan, of course, was strikingly new to California politics. His face and name were familiar through movies and television, but always in good guy roles. He had the aura of the celebrity about him. Instead of boredom, the people felt a curiosity about this "new politician."

In contrast to 1962, when Nixon was bloodied in a Republican primary fight with Joseph Shell, Reagan coasted to an easy victory over former San Francisco Mayor George Christopher, in the 1966 primary. The brilliant GOP State Chairman of that year, Gaylord Parkinson, had also successfully established what he called the "Eleventh Commandment" in the Republican Party and campaigns: "Thou shalt not speak ill of any Republican." There were deep divisions within the Republican Party philosophically, and sharp personal antagonisms between some of its leading figures, but Reagan, Parkinson, and others managed to create an impression of harmony and unity. Their method was simple. They screamed at each other and hammered out their differences behind closed doors, then came out to face the cameras for arm-in-arm "unity" press conferences.

The Democratic Party in California offered the opposite impression in 1966. We were becoming known as a party of squabblers, fighting among ourselves more for personal power and prerogative than for the public good. Democrats tended to rationalize their squabbles by proclaiming that the arguments were out in the open, as befitting a free society. But, in fact, we tended to smile at each other and speak cordially behind closed doors, then one among us would step outside to face the cameras and blast away at his fellow-Democrats. The apolitical California public was impatient with the well-publicized fights between such Democratic leaders as myself and Assembly Speaker Jess Unruh. (Unruh was a close and respected ally during my first term as Governor. His brilliant legislative generalship was largely responsible for the success of many of my programs. But, during my second term, he directed many of his fighter instincts toward me and was openly antagonistic and privately uncooperative. Perhaps because of his impatience to become Governor, he seemed determined to make my governmental and political life so unpleasant that I would decide not to run for re-election.) Lurking behind many of the problems and divisions within the Democratic Party in California was the increasingly anguished issue of the Vietnam war. It tore us apart as much in 1966 as it divided the party nationally in 1968.

I faced the November election after a stiff primary fight with Los Angeles Mayor Sam Yorty. There was no "Eleventh Commandment" in the Democratic Party. Yorty, who had won a substantial vote in the primary, continued his attacks on me and was openly friendly to Reagan. Usually described as a "maverick Democrat," Yorty is a Democrat in registration only. He supported Richard Nixon over John Kennedy in 1960, and generally takes delight in insulting or sabotaging the efforts of Democratic leaders. The enmity between us contributed to the public impression of Democratic division, in contrast to GOP harmony.

The deep social and racial tensions that were emerging in California in 1966 were cleverly exploited by Reagan to his advantage as a candidate; I emerged as the scapegoat. Reagan and other Republicans painted the Democratic state administration as "soft" on black violence, student riots, and general lawlessness. There was intensified public resistance to government spending in California in 1966, and Reagan pinned the blame for increasing governmental costs on Democratic "irresponsibility" and not on the actual growth of the state. California was also one of the first major political battlegrounds of the "Law 'n Order" issue. Reagan proclaimed, "We must preserve and enforce law and order." Period. I also emphasized the need for tough law enforcement and could back up my position with a solid record in that field during my years as Governor, State Attorney General, and San Francisco District Attorney. My firm position on law enforcement, however, was aligned with an equally outspoken position on the need for society and government to reduce the *conditions* of poverty and injustice, which increased crime. I was identified clearly as favoring and establishing policies and programs (Fair Employment Practices, Fair Housing laws, and others) of "equal opportunity" and "social justice." Tragically, such concepts were out of style politically in 1966. Californians were turned off by such words as "compassion" and "understanding" following ghetto violence or student turmoil. Confused, fearful, or threatened, they did not want any qualifications added to the simple call for tough law enforcement. They wanted a candidate to set his jaw firmly, pound his fist on the rostrum, and demand, without qualification or elaboration, "Law 'n Order." Reagan offered that firm stance and promise in the campaign of 1966.

Another major, underlying change in society partially accounted for Reagan's victory in California in 1966, and, I believe, Nixon's victory nationally in 1968. In essence, the Democratic Party has contributed to its own defeats in recent years by helping to create an affluent society. For more than thirty years, the Democratic Party aligned itself with and sought to advance the cause of the underdog in the nation— the poor, the suppressed minorities, the struggling worker, and the intellectuals who allied themselves with the disadvantaged. After three decades of policies, programs, and budgets, the Democratic Party had helped to broaden affluence in the nation, particularly in California, and reduce, numerically, the biggest source of its political strength. Today there are fewer poor, the blacks and other minorities have made substantial advances socially, and the "struggling" worker has two cars in the garage and a boat in the driveway. The underdogs of the nation, even with their intellectual allies, no longer comprise anywhere near a political majority. Democrats retain a substantial edge over Republicans in formal voter registration (the margin is more than a million and a half in California), but the registration figures are becoming meaningless in the moment of truth when citizens move into the booth to vote their feelings and opinions. California and the nation are still blemished by pockets of poverty and groups of underdogs, but the increased militancy of the poor, the blacks, and their student allies has antagonized the majority of affluent, tax-paying voters. Politically, the American underdog is today passé. When his hair is long or worn in Afro-style, he is, in the mind of the majority, downright repulsive. At least on the surface and publicly, the Democratic Party has continued to identify itself with the underdog and to commit itself to spending the money—taxpayers' money—to give the underdog greater opportunity. The result was evident to me in California in 1966 and nationally in 1968 and now: In terms of the surface attitudes and opinions of the people, the Democratic Party today is the *minority* party in California and the nation.

In 1966 a majority of Californians wanted to hear a new articulation of their changed political and social attitudes. Ronald Reagan masterfully articulated the new complaints, fears, antagonisms and suspicions of that majority. He gave the majority not only a collective voice, but also an open respectability to views that it wasn't quite sure were acceptable in the context of American values. Sometimes explicitly, sometimes by strong implication, Reagan offered a clear good guys–bad guys distinction in the campaign of 1966. "They" were the criminals and hoodlums, the restless blacks and the impatient students, the lazy professors and vacillating campus administrators, the cynical politicians and the spending Governors. "We" were the law-abiding, tax-paying, patriotic, nonpolitical, long-suffering, and mostly white middle class who wanted to return to a simpler, nicer, and more orderly time. Often wearing an electric-blue suit and constantly reminding his audiences of his skilled horsemanship, Ronald Reagan rode into power in Sacramento as a sort of McLuhanesque cowboy, ready to rid the state of the modern bandits and troublemakers.

There are two great ironies in the Reagan campaign of 1966 and his subsequent performance as Governor of California.

The first is that, for all his belligerent negativism, his antigovernment attitudes, and his emphasis on the wrongs of the world, Reagan came across to the majority of Californians as a *positive* man. Unlike his earlier political hero, Barry Goldwater, Reagan never suffered from a reputation of shoot-from-the-hip negativism. Philosophically and politically, Reagan *is* a negative figure, pouring his energies into attempts to denounce, restrain, or cut back. But personally, Reagan somehow conveys an impression of positiveness. To many Californians, his voice is sincere, and his actions seem cloaked in genuine conviction. His manner is that of a man with utter confidence in his own fundamentalist purity and integrity. At times, he offers the image of an efficient missionary dedicated to eradicating the evils that are beleaguering our society and lives. Even his banal campaign slogan, "The Creative Society," conveyed the notion that he was out to build something good and not just tear down the bad. I remain convinced that Ronald Reagan is a negative figure and force in society and government, but a majority of Californians have regarded him as a positive personality.

The second irony of Reagan is that, for all his expressed contempt for politics and politicians, he is an instinctively talented and increasingly skilled politician. Very possibly he would regard the label "politician" as an insult. The fact is that Reagan *is* a politician of extraordinary talent. In 1966, he correctly read, sensed, understood, and knew the public mood and what the people of California wanted, I, whom he scornfully called a politician, was not as discerning, perceptive, and skilled in that political campaign as he was. There can be no definitive, all-inclusive definition of what politics is, but mastery of politics must include the achievements of getting elected, influencing a majority of the people, and sustaining personal popularity. Reagan has achieved all three.

But politics, at least during election campaigns, is, in a sense, the art of the superficial. Reagan was extraordinarily talented in that art during the campaign of 1966. In a state where televised images are powerful politically, Reagan's television image and method were flawless. In a time when the people were frustrated and confused by revolutionary social change and hungered for comforting capsules of hope, Reagan's simple aphorisms were persuasive and appealing.

Ronald Reagan, I am eager to acknowledge, is undoubtedly a sincere man. I also believe that he is in reality what he appears to be: a simple man. His ideas, his philosophy, his perceptions, his comprehension of human affairs and society are all neatly confined to a simple framework of thought and action, which permits no doubts and acknowledges no sobering complexities. "I think there *are* simple answers to California's problems," Reagan said again and again in the 1966 campaign. That statement, and his basically simplistic stance on all the issues and crises confronting

California, were immensely appealing to a people troubled by rapid and sometimes violent social change.

But it is one thing to be a successful candidate and popular personality, and another to be an effective Governor—particularly in this diverse, changing, and complex state. In the moments of truth when a Governor sits in the corner office of the State Capitol and must, by a sweep of the pen or nod of the head, decide complex issues and difficult questions, the lives and the futures of people hang in the balance. That is not a simple responsibility. In the final reality of leadership and public authority, a Governor needs more than a smile and a quip to govern wisely and well.

It also takes something far different than inflammatory remarks by a Governor to resolve today's social conflicts. On April 7, 1970, Reagan revealed the truly dangerous essence of his simplistic attitudes with a frightening statement made at a luncheon meeting in Yosemite Valley. Answering a question about campus disorders, he said that student militants are "part and parcel of revolution," and then added:

"If it takes a bloodbath, let's get it over with. No more appeasement."

Shocked newsmen caught up with Reagan later and challenged him on the statement. The Governor recanted only slightly. He said the phrase was just "a figure of speech, I wasn't even aware I had used." But then he declared, "There must come a moment when we bite the bullet so to speak, to take action when action is needed. You can't worry about radicalizing more students. You must face them."

Reagan's press secretary, Paul Beck, tried harder to soften the impact of the Governor's grisly statement. "He wasn't even aware he said it," Beck lamely explained about the "bloodbath" remark. "I don't think anyone in his right mind would say he wanted a bloodbath."

I agree.

2

A Style of Simplicity

In any careful analysis of Ronald Reagan's record as Governor, it is difficult to find any policy or program that is truly creative or original. The unbroken thread running through the fabric of his "Creative Society" is a dull, simplistic recitation of fundamentally conservative values and conventional, conservative wisdom. Even when I have forced myself to assume an open mind and neutral perspective, I could find only one, small innovation in the Reagan Governorship. He and his staff call it the "mini-memo."

The mini-memo is a startlingly original device the Reagan Administration has created to simplify the complex task of leadership. As devised by his former chief assistant William Clark, Jr., and explained by his staff, the mini-memo works this way:

When a political, legislative, social, or economic issue requires a decision by the Governor, his staff prepares a *one-*

page summary of all its aspects, concluding with a suggested decision. It is divided neatly into four succinct paragraphs, one each for The Issue, The Facts, The Discussion, and The Recommendation. There is enough space at the bottom of the page for Reagan to pen a check mark to indicate either "yes" or "no" on the recommendation for action.

He and his staff have boasted about the mini-memo as the ultimately efficient method by which the Governor becomes informed and through which he decides. They have maintained that there is no issue facing the Governor of California that can't be boiled down to a one-page summary and vehicle for decision-making. They have, when pressed by incredulous reporters, stated that sometimes Reagan does spend longer periods for "discussion" of an issue.

Brevity is often appropriate in the attempt to condense, digest, and understand masses of information, and it is possible that some variation of the mini-memo could be one, but only one, useful informational technique for a Governor. What is frightening about the Reagan mini-memo is the near singular reliance his administration places on it and the extent to which it represents the broader attitude by Reagan that there are quick and simple answers to the complex questions of government and society.

With the insights of eight years as Governor of California, I shudder at the thought that many problems now flowing to the Governor's desk are resolved after examination of one page prepared by a staff member, perhaps a few minutes of discussion, and a cocksure attitude of what is right and wrong. The decisions of a Governor are not just expressions of his personal philosophy or exercises in some game of politics. Those decisions affect—sometimes profoundly or critically—the lives of human beings. How could any conscientious man easily decide, after glancing at a one-page summary, whether or not to grant clemency to an individual who is scheduled to die in San Quentin's gas chamber? How could one page sum up the merits and weaknesses in a proposal to spend millions of dollars for some new and untested program to feed the hungry, or train the unemployed, or care for the sick? How could the questions involving the deep conflicts between races and the explosive challenges of the young be understood by the reading of a mini-memo?

Apparently Reagan thinks he can pull it off. I know that, as Governor, I couldn't. My technique in gathering information to prepare for decisions was varied, never simple or quick, and seldom completely satisfactory to me. There was no device comparable to the mini-memo in the operation of my office. I respected the intelligence, abilities, loyalty, and fairness of my staff assistants and other administration officials but never blindly trusted their reports and recommendations. If an assistant mentioned a newspaper or magazine article bearing on my duties, I invariably asked for a full copy to read myself. If a cabinet member offered a condensation of an important departmental report, I usually asked for a full copy, even while knowing that I would have to spend precious hours wading through legalistic gobbledygook or technical jargon to assess its validity. If one expert in a particular area or one trusted adviser came to me with a confident and unqualified recommendation, I was inclined to accept it, but would then call in another expert or adviser to ask, "What do you think?"

My style of operating as Governor rarely allowed a serene, eight-hour work day in the corner office of the State Capitol; ten or eleven hours in that office was typical. Reagan is a 9-A.M.-to-6-P.M. Governor. Nor did my method permit any semblance of a normal private life. The briefcase I carried home each night was always full, and I considered it a luxury to steal a half hour to watch the late night news on television.

My habit of taking time—on some issues a *long* time—to reach a decision and to ask innumerable individuals "What do you think I ought to do?" contributed to a part of my reputation that was a disadvantage at election time. I was, in the minds of some reporters and many voters, "indecisive."

In retrospect, I realize that I lacked the Reagan knack for the quick quip or comment that gives an impression of decisiveness. In fact, my political eclipse resulted more from the firm decisions I reached and fought for than the sometimes lengthy, questioning, publicly unsure process of reaching a decision. After years of hard study and thought on California's water needs, for example, I decided that an immensely expensive project was needed to carry water from northern California to the growing, thirsty population of southern California. Many powerful interests and innumerable voters didn't like the California water plan, for a variety of reasons, but I pushed it through. At times, I was indeed indecisive on an issue that involved a personal, philosophical conflict. An example was the Chessman case, a tragically long situation involving a man who was under sentence to die in the gas chamber. Personally, I am opposed to capital punishment; that conviction stems from my own moral and religious values. Legally, however, I was bound, as Governor, to uphold the law; as a lawyer and former Attorney General, I respected the obligation for a Governor to carry out the decisions of the courts. But, in the Chessman case, moral and legal questions were intricate and controversial. I wavered for a time (as did many other conscientious legal authorities) until Caryl Chessman died in the gas chamber in 1962. The public was vividly aware of my "indecisiveness" that year, but I was still able to defeat Richard Nixon in the 1962 gubernatorial election. (For all the personal and political difficulties of the Chessman case, I felt that I acted honestly and properly. In retrospect now, I would not have acted differently.) In 1964, I was firmly and publicly "decisive" in my support of an open housing law, which had passed the State Legislature but was rejected by the voters. My decision to fight for that law, the Rumford Act, extended beyond 1964, and I bluntly labeled as bigots the real estate interests who were fighting it. With increasing racial tensions, white backlash, and fear in 1965 and 1966, such decisive support for the Rumford Open Housing Act (which was sustained by the state and national Supreme Courts) was not popular. I have concluded that it was decisiveness on such issues that, in large measure, defeated me in 1966, not any public impatience over my time-consuming, questioning struggles with some of the tough issues.

There is a paradox that emerges in a careful study of Reagan's performance as Governor. Publicly and personally, he gives the impression of a simple, comfortable, and confident decisiveness; there is seldom any doubt by most of the voters that Reagan is sure about what is right or wrong and that he is on the right side. But substantively and as Governor, he is often ambivalent, inconsistent, evasive, and indecisive. That's what is perhaps most distressing, for anyone who is concerned about the health of representative, democratic government, about Reagan's significance as a successful politician today. The scary thing about the man is the immense gap, if not the clear contradiction, between the public's *impression* of what he is and the *reality* of what he is doing as Governor.

Richard Nixon's Presidential Administration represents, somewhat less clearly, the same gap between public impression and actual reality of leadership. When I read that one of President Nixon's top assistants told a reporter, "Don't pay any attention to what we say; just watch what we do," I shuddered again about the bleak prospects for democracy in America. If our top leaders, our Governors and Presidents, completely separate their public roles from their substantive actions, how can the people know them, judge them, and vote wisely?

The record of Reagan as Governor offers abundant and glaring examples of contradictions between what he says and what he does. The most profound gap can be seen in the area of government finance and economy. He won election, in part, because of his charges of fiscal irresponsibility, reckless spending, and rising governmental costs during my administrations, and he repeatedly pledged to "cut, trim, and squeeze" to keep government costs down. Opinion polls indicate that a large majority of Californians have the impression that Reagan has succeeded in keeping budgets and taxes down. In fact, Reagan came through with the biggest tax increase ($1 billion) in the history of any state in the nation. The amounts and the rates of his yearly budget increases have exceeded the annual increases in the budgets of my two administrations. But, through some talent of rhetoric, Reagan has remained identified as a tight-fisted "economy" Governor.

Another gap between the impression and the reality of Reagan's performance emerges clearly in the pattern of his appointments. In his 1966 campaign, Reagan promised that only "the most qualified persons" would be appointed by him to public office, and he charged that I had "repeatedly violated this principle by selecting political cronies, hacks, and defeated Democratic candidates to fill important positions." Once in office, Reagan blithely made the following appointments: his own personal attorney, William French Smith, to the University of California Board of Regents; his campaign airplane pilot, Mervine Amerine, to the State Aeronautics Board; his personal barber, Vincent P. Cicone, to the State Board of Barber Examiners; the only defeated Republican candidate for statewide office, Spencer Williams, to head the State Welfare Department. When one reporter noted that more than 80 per cent of Reagan's judicial appointments were Republicans and asked about his pledges for nonpartisan appointments, Reagan replied, "It's just a remarkable coincidence that some of the most qualified people available happened to be in my campaign."

Sacramento newsmen often leave his press conferences

feeling that the Governor has spoken clearly and decisively on some issues. Then, examining their notes or the verbatim transcript, they discover that his words were noncommital. In his press conference of March 5, 1968, Reagan offered a long statement praising the old Civilian Conservation Corps and leaving a distinct impression that he favored a similar program, at the state level, to put unemployed young men to work on conservation projects. But when reporters studied the transcript, this is what they found:

REAGAN: ". . . It is a job that could be done if you had the facilities and the means to do it. Now, in our own summer jobs, we are thinking in terms of fire trails and the stepping up of a program of hiking trails in our wilderness areas and so forth. . . ."

QUESTIONER: "This sort of thing requires money, though, Governor. Have you allocated anything in your budget to it?"

REAGAN: "As I said, we are looking at that one. . . ."

On some issues, usually those that have already aroused public wrath, Reagan is not at all vague. Unfortunately, his simplistic and rigidly moralistic judgments frequently involve the most sensitive and volatile problems facing the state and the nation.

Some of Reagan's remarks make Spiro T. Agnew seem like an inarticulate milquetoast by comparison. Commenting on the tragic, complicated, and still simmering pattern of Negro ghetto riots in July, 1967, Reagan said, "These are no longer riots connected with civil rights in any way. These are riots of the lawbreakers and the mad dogs against the people." In October, 1967, Reagan was asked about labor union leaders who had complained about the use of state prisoners to harvest crops, and he answered this way: "Sometimes they remind me of, you know, a dog sitting on a sharp rock howling with pain [and who] is too stupid to get up." Angered by the late columnist Drew Pearson's charges of a scandal involving Reagan's staff, the Governor said that Pearson "had better not spit on the sidewalk if he returns to California."

To some extent, I sympathize with any Governor or public official whose occasional verbal bloopers are joyfully played up in the press. Reagan is still trying to live down one comment he made several years ago during a controversy over the size of a proposed national park for northern California's redwood groves. He was quoted as saying, "If you've seen one tree, you've seen them all." There are moments, in the furious pace of an election campaign or in the flurry of questioning at a press conference, when the words don't come out quite as the speaker intends. I'm still trying to live down a comment I made about a series of devastating floods in northern California several years ago: "This is the worst disaster in California since my election as Governor."

A slip of the tongue is excusable, but a cynically or carelessly simplistic statement on a sensitive public issue is unpardonable. One of the most sensitive and volatile issues facing society in recent years has been the pattern of student unrest, demonstrations, and occasional violence. The pattern began in California and for at least three years has been acute on the state's campuses. Where the crisis of campus unrest cried out for calm, firm, but fair comment and leadership, Reagan chose instead to play the role of an indignant propagandist. His angry rhetoric, I believe, added as much to campus turmoil as the excesses of radical campus agitators.

An example involves the tragic People's Park controversy at Berkeley in the spring of 1969. That was an immensely complicated situation involving the unauthorized use, by students and local youth, of a university owned vacant lot. In May, several hundred young people began planting sod and other greenery to transform the parcel into a park. The university, acting narrowly but within its legal rights, ordered construction of a fence to keep the young out and to end the work. As a result of general indignation, cynical agitation by some of the youths, and inefficient or undisciplined law enforcement tactics, violence erupted—leaving one man dead, another blinded, more than 200 injured, and several hundred arrested.

University Chancellor Roger Heyns, some of the students, and many of the law enforcement personnel tried desperately to calm the violent emotions and to inject some reason into the escalating passions on the People's Park issue.

Reagan's official authority in the controversy was limited. He did act properly when, on the request of local leaders, he imposed a curfew in Berkeley and called out the National Guard to help restore order. But, at the most volatile moments of the crisis, he also fanned the passions by references to the need for "bayonets" to quell the turmoil, by condemnation of harried university administrators as "appeasers," and by blanket indictments of all those who supported the People's Park project—idealistic environmentalists as well as radical agitators—as "the mob."

I am no less critical than Reagan of the violence-advocating militants on campuses or anywhere else, and I am personally committed to the prompt use of law enforcement personnel to control riots. But a political leader in today's free American society is not just a Commander-in-Chief whose only duty is to shout "Charge!" when segments of the society challenge authority. That, in essence, is all that Reagan did in the People's Park tragedy. In any volatile social upheaval, a Governor's public stance and statements will tend either to enflame or to calm passions. In today's restless society, one of the key responsibilities of the public leader is to serve as a conciliator of conflicting groups. Reagan is more intent on picking one side and fighting with it.

His one definitive statement on the People's Park tragedy was more of a battle cry than an attempt to calm the crisis and create public understanding of the issues involved. On June 13, 1969, in an address to the Commonwealth Club in San Francisco, he ignored the complex issues involved, carelessly or cynically perverted the facts to suit his belligerent viewpoint, and denied, except in the most abstract terms, that students and youth generally had *any* legitimate grievances against the bureaucratic behemoth of Berkeley. That speech was a stark example of Reagan's "good guys–bad guys" perspective toward all social and human conflict.

The people deserve basic honesty and fairness from their Governor when he speaks out on a crisis. Reagan misled the people in his Commonwealth Club address on People's Park. Here are just a few samples:

REAGAN: "At no time did the squatters [on the university-owned lot] even designate an individual or a committee with whom the Chancellor could communicate."

FACT: Student Body President Charles Palmer repeatedly contacted the Chancellor to discuss the crisis, and, on May 14, the People's Park advocates did form a committee to negotiate with the university.

REAGAN: "Now it has been learned that part of the lush greenery that was planted to make the lot a so-called sylvan glade turned out to be marijuana."

FACT: Neither the police nor any other authority produced evidence that marijuana plants were growing in People's Park.

REAGAN: "There are no shortages of parks in Berkeley."

FACT: At the time of the People's Park turmoil, there was no park at all serving the huge south campus area jammed with high-rise student residences and private dwellings. The Berkeley City Council acknowledged the lack of open space and park facilities in the area.

REAGAN: "The symptoms of [student] rebellion have been evident for some time. They no longer bother to vote in student elections."

FACT: In a special referendum on the People's Park issue, more students (14,969) students voted than in any election in the university's history. And 85 per cent of them supported the "unauthorized" People's Park development.

Reagan's simplistic, gung-ho, side-choosing attitude is tragic enough in such local and state crises as the People's Park situation. The same attitude, if applied to national or international crises, is frightening to contemplate. All Americans should consider that prospect, for the reason that any Governor of California—the largest state in the nation—is automatically a serious possibility as a candidate for the Presidency or Vice Presidency of the United States. Reagan himself, for all his coy public statements, was in fact an eager and "serious" contender for the GOP Presidential nomination in 1968—and it could happen again in 1972 or 1976.

His simplistic, good guys–bad guys attitudes extend to the delicate, international life-and-death issues in this nuclear age. In the same manner that he sees the students of Berkeley as the enemy and is inclined to scream "Charge!" when any of them challenge the existing order, he reacts quickly and impulsively to international conflict. It was personally difficult for me to see Reagan take over the authority of California's state government and, in subsequent years, halt the progress of the state and accelerate its social conflicts. But, as a human being and an American who is deeply concerned about peace and survival in this nuclear age, I am chilled to the bone at the possibility of Ronald Reagan some day becoming President of the United States. Several times in the past few years, he has publicly, explicitly, and firmly equated the possible use of U.S. nuclear weapons with the firing of muskets at Concord Bridge at the onset of the American Revolution. "There comes a time," he said, in the context of a discussion about the potential use of nuclear weapons, "when we have to take a stand against the Communists." All of our recent Presidents and most citizens who have spent any time at all thinking about the destructive power of nuclear weapons regard their potential use with extreme caution. Not Reagan. When questioned about some actual or implicit threat from Communist nations, Reagan usually invokes an obscure, parenthetical, out-of-context quote from Dwight D. Eisenhower to the effect that we ought to make the enemy believe and fear that we are ready and eager to use nuclear weapons.

It does not require much imagination to know how Reagan would react to some international threat or crisis. In early 1968, the U.S. intelligence vessel *Pueblo* was captured by the North Koreans. For a brief time, America debated the facts and issues involved. Ultimately, and after patient, tedious, and delicate negotiations, the captured crew members of the *Pueblo* were safely returned home and an open, armed conflict with North Korea was avoided.

How would a President Reagan have handled the delicate *Pueblo* crisis? The answer is revealed in his press conference of January 30, 1968:

QUESTION: "Governor, a few days ago you were quoted as saying that you would have given North Korea twenty-four hours to release the *Pueblo* and prove that we were going to go in and get it. I wonder if you would clarify for us whether under the circumstances you would anticipate armed resistance . . . and if so whether this would endanger the lives of the eighty-three [crew members]. . . ."

REAGAN: "Well, first of all, no one wants to endanger the lives of the eighty-three. . . . I think that what we are ignoring in this climate of recent years is the moral obligation, the sacred obligation of government to protect any individual, wherever he may be in the world, if his rights are being unjustly imposed upon by someone else. That's the purpose of government, to provide the strength of the collective citizenry to go to the aid of any one of us. And now it is the aid of eighty-three of us—and I said, twenty-four hours. . . . There is no moral justification for this country standing by and letting what amounts to an act of piracy, an act of war, be perpetrated upon us and write off eighty-three young men. . . ."

QUESTIONER: "My question was, Governor, that if you've made the ultimatum we are going in to get them, what would you anticipate happening? Would the eighty-three still be alive for us to rescue? Would you want to bomb the port where the ship sits? Take the city by force?"

REAGAN: "You are asking for specifics that I've just told you I don't think anyone can give who doesn't have access to the advice of the Chiefs of Staff about such an incident. But if you are going to be overly concerned . . . as to whether the enemy is going to retaliate in any way—when they are in truth the criminal, they are guilty—then I'd like to ask what number do we set the limit on? How many of our citizens can be kidnapped by a foreign power before the rest of us decide that they have reached a point in which we have an obligation to do something about it. . . . I do know what the limit is in my mind. I think the limit is one. . . ."

QUESTIONER: "Can I phrase it just one more time? Then do you think it is possible to get back our eighty-three men forcibly without a very dire jeopardy of their lives?"

REAGAN: "Yes, yes, I do. . . ."

QUESTIONER: "Governor, do you find the President's conduct thus far in the entire incident bordering on appeasement?"

REAGAN: "I think it is a continuation of a policy of appeasement that started a long time ago. . . ."

The drama of the influence of a Governor is perhaps less pronounced than the authority of a President, in this nuclear age. The world may well go on, man may well survive if a Governor of California exercises the wrong influences or makes the wrong decisions. But individual human beings— thousands or millions of them—*are* influenced in their attitudes and affected in their lives by the statements and actions of a Governor.

Governor Ronald Reagan, by his simplistic statements, is today profoundly influencing the political attitudes of most Californians—which they will hold and vote upon for a long time. His decisions and judgments—on policy, programs, and budgets—will affect their lives for a long time.

I believe that Reagan's statements and judgments are basically destructive in a society of complex, growing, changing needs. To me, and to those who carefully examine his words and actions, he is a negative factor in the progress of democracy, a negative force in the future of California.

California and its problems are complex; Reagan and his attitudes are simple. The state and the man are in conflict. Why then was he elected, and why then does he remain popular?

The prime reason stems from the new political power of television.

3

Two-dimensional Politics

The nature of politics has changed in the past two decades. I fondly remember my first campaigns in the 1940's and early 1950's, when I followed the advice of former Governor Earl Warren to visit the town squares and county courthouses, talking on a man-to-man level with the people. In that earlier time—or in smaller states today—politics could be a pleasantly personal human activity. A candidate could see and be seen by enough individuals to make the difference between victory and defeat in an election. He knew that his time was well spent when he spoke with a few hundred individuals each day; they would return to their neighborhoods to share their impressions with friends. Through most of American history, this direct, personal contact between the politician and the people was an essential element of political campaigns.

Not any more. Particularly in California, with a population of 20 million, "stump" campaigning is an exercise in futility, an obsolete technique that lingers more from habit than from political practicality. With almost 10 million registered voters, a candidate cannot expect to influence the outcome of an election through person-to-person contact. Most statewide candidates in California accept this sad truth, but they generally persist in "touring" the state during campaigns—shaking hands, standing at factory gates, visiting shopping centers, and offering speeches to clusters of voters in town halls, city auditoriums, and hotel ballrooms. Even when such tours are perfectly organized and the auditoriums are filled with attentive voters, there is little direct benefit, in terms of votes gained, from the exercise. Political rallies today are attended largely by those who are already committed and friendly to the speaker. Most Californians, worn out after the evening freeway battle to get home, don't have the time or the inclination to go out again to hear a visiting politician boast about his freeway program.

Person-to-person campaigning continues, even in California, for a variety of purposes, each of them related only indirectly to the task of winning an election. One purpose is to "fire up the troops"—meaning campaign staffs and volunteer workers. The stump speech, if cleverly or imaginatively staged, is also a device to attract attention from a press and public that seem increasingly bored with the substance of candidates' statements. It is also part of a now vital segment of any major campaign, the fund-raising dinner. Soaring campaign costs have created the necessity for a new political ritual—the $100- (or $500- or $1,000-) a-plate dinner. But even at these events, the candidate's speech is scheduled at the end of the program almost as an afterthought; the black-tie guests spend most of the evening munching filet mignon, congratulating each other for their good citizenship, and being entertained by local or Hollywood celebrities. I was always grateful for the help of such Hollywood figures as Gregory Peck, Frank Sinatra, Dean Martin, and Rowan and Martin, but they were tough acts to follow at fund-raising dinners.

(The influence of Hollywood on California's politics and society is usually exaggerated by national observers. Many entertainers participate effectively in political campaigns and are intelligently interested in government, but their talents do not dominate the campaigns in the way that the guitar-strumming and folk-singing in many deep-South campaigns do. The more subtle Hollywood influences—emphasizing attractive physical appearance—simply blend in with the era of television, which is a national phenomenon.)

Incumbent political leaders, in particular, have another and more personal reason for person-to-person campaigning. Psychologically, they need and want the direct contact with constituents. After months or years of political insulation in office, a politician wants to break away from the statistical and seemingly abstract questions to see and touch human beings in their own environments. Person-to-person campaigning, for a particular kind of politician, can be fun. After confinement to controversy and criticism in public office, the smiles, friendliness, and applause of citizens can be a positive morale-booster for a lonely President, Governor, or Mayor.

I liked political campaigning, particularly the portions of it devoted to direct contact with the people. It is difficult to describe why, and I suppose I risk giving the impression of corny sentimentality when I say that I simply enjoy people and contact with them. I always found it stimulating to move quickly from place to place and town to town in California to meet with new people, as individuals and in groups. The campaign experience always gave me a new awareness of the infinite diversity of personalities and view-points that make up the California constituency, and always refreshed my knowledge that the problems I was facing as Governor were human problems.

There are, of course, some disadvantages to the old and fading style of stump campaigning. It has involved a lot of silly and superficial aspects; I disliked wearing outlandish hats or being adorned and stuffed with locally produced offerings. The stump style of campaigning, in a state as large as California, can be physically exhausting, reducing the candidate, at times, to a mechanical spouting of clichés and, at other times, to a groggy confusion about where he is. I recall one example of the latter mood in the 1962 gubernatorial campaign. After one particular week of non-stop driving, flying, speaking, hand-shaking, and late-night strategy sessions with local leaders, I fell into a deep sleep in a motel room in a small town in California's central valley. Still tired and somewhat dazed when I woke in the morning, I was in one of those "Where am I?" moods for a few moments. Suddenly I became aware that a female was in bed next to me. Near panic, I thought, "My God, Nixon's people are framing me—they have slipped some woman into my bed," and I expected photographers to rush in at any instant to document this immoral and politically devastating scene. Then the fog cleared, I recognized my wife, Bernice, and realized that, in the exhaustion and confusion, I had forgotten that she had joined me the previous evening.

Despite the disadvantages of stump campaigning, I remained aware that it was a healthy part of the democratic political process. With all its silliness and superficiality, the person-to-person campaign brings a sense of reality to the relationship between constituents and candidate. When they see and listen to each other, the candidate realizes that the people are not some abstraction loosely related to the problems and decisions of government; the people realize that the candidate is not some heroic, larger-than-life creature. Direct exposure of a candidate to the people adds depth— the third dimension—to their understanding of him.

That dimension and value is lost, to a large extent, in the new and necessary reliance by candidates on the mass media, particularly television. In California, television is not just one technique and medium of communication and politics. Its direct and subtle influences dominate the state's politics, far more than newspapers.

It is difficult for the prototypical American politician, conditioned by years of direct contact with the people, to adjust to the new political milieu of television. He is a proud man, who winces when experts spread makeup over his face and tell him what to say. He operates partly by instinct, hunch, and empathy and does not like the invasion of technology into his imprecise realm. He is exuberant in the midst of crowds of human beings but is depressed by the metallic and pasteboard clutter of television studios. He needs to see the faces, or at least sense the mood, of the audience; now he must gaze at the glass eye of the camera and respond to the clinical curiosity of the men of the mass media. Instead of speaking from his heart, he must now read from the electrically controlled teleprompter placed just above the camera. With a pragmatic attitude and proper coaching, the prototypical politician can cope with the new milieu of television, but he resents the middlemen and machines separating him from the people.

Ronald Reagan relishes the new two-dimensional politics of television. He represents not a new breed of politician but is rather a natural example of a new and radically different type of politics. Two-dimensional politics, the result of television, is now firmly established in California; it is also becoming the new politics nationally. The prime characteristic of the new two-dimensional politics is the dominance of the simple, surface *appearance* of men and human affairs, rather than the deeply complex realities of humanity.

Reagan is an artist of today's two-dimensional politics. He is adept and natural in this new political realm as a result of both his professional experience as a motion picture and television actor and his personal characteristics as a man. For almost thirty years, Reagan polished his acting talents in the movie and television studios of Hollywood, never attaining the first rank of his profession but achieving a comfortable competence in front of the cameras. (When first informed that Reagan might run for Governor, his former boss, Jack Warner, replied, "No. Jimmy Stewart for Governor. Ronnie for Best Friend.") For two-dimensional politics, Reagan is also blessed with surface features that are immediately appealing: a resonant voice with a tone of natural sincerity and just the right touch of boyishness, a hairline as unmoving as the Maginot Line, and a ruggedly handsome face that is neither unusual enough to jar the viewer nor so deeply wrinkled that it can't be smoothed out with make-up. He will be sixty years old in 1971—the same age as Hubert H. Humphrey—but most Californians would probably guess, on the basis of *appearance,* that he is ten to fifteen years younger than the former Vice President.

Many politicians who were accustomed to the more traditional, personal methods of campaigns are today deeply concerned about what they call "packaged politics"—the process by which the candidate is placed completely in the hands of image-making experts and, with little chance to assert his own identity, presented to the voters as an attractive package. Reagan, I am sure, does not share the concern. He *is* the package. He arrived on the California political scene already possessing the neat, colorful, and attractive wrappings that would delight any public relations profes-

sional. The anxious question many of us ask is whether or
not there is anything *inside* the Reagan package. Is the most
important reality and identity of the man the attractive
wrapping itself, the surface appearance? Appropriately, I
think, Reagan titled his autobiography of a few years ago
Where Is the Rest of Me? If he doesn't know, how can anyone else, including the voters, be expected to know what's
behind the attractive wrapping of the Reagan package?

There is nothing wrong, of course, with an actor running
for or winning public office, and I am not suggesting that a
candidate should be suspect because he has a handsome
face. Some of the complaints of traditional politicians against
younger, handsome candidates represent a silly form of
prejudice. But Americans should at least consider some of
the possible consequences of the extent to which two-dimensional politics favors the superficially attractive candidate.
The pattern is already evident: A quick glance at the pictures
of most of the newly elected Governors, Senators, and Mayors
in recent years reveals a striking similarity of attractive physical features. Speaking frankly for a moment as one politician
whose face was most often characterized as "owlish," I admit
a degree of pettiness when I suggest that many of the newly
successful candidates remind me of the models for magazine
advertisements promoting men's hair tonic.

As the new two-dimensional politics places more and more
emphasis on a candidate's superficial features, California and
the nation stand to lose many potentially excellent and brilliant public leaders. Sadly, I expect that politically inclined
men of extraordinary integrity, intelligence, honesty, skill,
and talent may well be rejected by the new politics primarily
because of some inconsequential feature such as an oversized
nose or unusually bushy eyebrows. Reluctantly, I suspect
that, if a modern Abraham Lincoln appeared today, he probably couldn't be elected Mayor of Springfield, Illinois; with

his gauntly homely face, he wouldn't even be considered for high state or national office in the current judgments of political experts. If an American version of Winston Churchill appeared in California today, he probably couldn't win election to the Los Angeles City Council; with his slight lisp and jowly, cherubic face, he'd do better to confine himself to writing history books and painting pastoral scenes.

The two-dimensional politics of television is transforming attitudes toward public issues as well as public personalities. With the new emphasis on the appearance—the superficial physical features—of individuals, Americans are being conditioned now to judge the worth of a cause less on its intrinsic merits than on the fashion of its advocates' clothes or their hair style. In 1963, the Civil Rights March in Washington was, for most Americans, a respectable, proper, moving demonstration by 100,000 individuals seeking progress in civil rights. There were many reasons for the respectability and success of the 1963 march. One, I am convinced, is the fact that the blacks and whites who demonstrated then were generally dressed in suits and ties and had orthodox haircuts. In 1969, even more people marched in the same spot in Washington demonstrating for a moratorium on the Vietnam war. There were many reasons for the fact that the 1969 Moratorium march was publicly unpopular in the country and did not result in any practical success. One reason, I'm sure, is that the television viewer saw blacks with high, free-growing Afro hair styles and young whites dressed in hippie-style clothes.

My own view is that the style in which an individual chooses to wear his hair should not affect any public judgment of the cause he espouses. But I am afraid that the new two-dimensional politics is conditioning Americans to make up their minds on the basis of their first, quick, superficial reactions to style and taste rather than rational consideration of facts and ideas. I think it's fair to say that, several years ago, the collective judgment of Americans toward race relations was significantly influenced by the peaceful, soft-spoken, neatly dressed Martin Luther King. Today, I am convinced, the average white American is significantly influenced in his attitudes by the image of an angry, violence-advocating, Black Panther.

This new emphasis on the mere appearance of candidates or the advocates of a cause is dangerous enough; the danger is compounded by television's adoption of the traditional definition of "news." The press has always considered the unusual and the violent events as news. Newspapers give far more space to murders than to concerts, far more attention to the mayhem of war than the serenity of peace, far more attention to the aberrations of the younger generation than the high school graduation ceremonies. For all its totally new style and effects, television has retained the news judgments of the older media. The cameras focus in on the ten, sack-dressed, long-haired, screaming demonstrators or hecklers in an auditorium, not on the thousand other individuals there who are listening politely to the speaker. And, of course, the cameras ignore the speaker even if the heckling is momentary and negligible in terms of the numbers of individuals involved. Partly because of television's hunger for conflict and the unusual, Martin Luther King was beginning to fade from public attention years before his assassination in 1968; the cameras, looking hungrily toward the new, the unusual, the graphic conflict, had begun to ignore the peaceful King and focus in on the speeches and actions of Stokely Carmichael and other angry black radicals.

I don't condemn the newsmen and executives of the television networks and stations. Both in their roles of public service and in their functions to provide public entertainment, they must avoid at all costs (and they are involved in a business) the cardinal sin of boring the people. The people, the viewers, by and large have spent tedious and boring hours during the day on the job or cleaning the house. During the evening hours and for news, they don't want and won't watch some repetition of the mundane, the peaceful. Their appetite for exciting conflict between distinctly antagonistic forces is keen.

Apparently, the television viewers want to watch or even perhaps vicariously experience conflict, but I doubt that they want to be involved personally in conflict, or the contentious problems of others. Americans today are a people who turn out in the millions to watch, from the comfort of the sidelines, a football game or some other form of detached conflict. We are also, apparently, a people who are afraid of getting involved in the problems of our neighbors—a reluctance dramatized a few years ago when dozens of New Yorkers idly watched or turned away while Kitty Genovese was being stabbed to death on the street; they didn't even bother to phone the police. I recall now a cynical bit of advice the Governor of another major state offered to me several years ago: "Don't be so conscientious as a Governor, Pat. You ought to go out and play golf every afternoon the way I do. Your trouble is that you spend too much time telling the people about problems, and sort of challenging them to *do* something themselves about the problems of society. The fact is that the people don't want to be bothered by big social problems. They have enough personal problems in their own lives already. Get off their backs, Pat. Leave them alone. If you don't ask them to get involved in the awesome problems of today's society, you'll probably get re-elected."

My fellow-Governor may have been right, in pragmatic political terms. I continued to challenge the people of California to become involved with the big problems of their state, to care personally and deeply about them, and to pay the taxes to help solve them. That stance—and I'm not suggesting it was the only reason for my defeat by Reagan—was imposing and unpopular with the voters of California in 1966.

Reagan is different. He does not challenge the people to become involved with the larger problems of their society. He doesn't appeal to their better instincts to be involved with the suffering and conflicts of their neighbors. He is the antithesis of the traditional political leader who sought to rally all the people into a concerted effort to solve some pressing human problem of society. Even as Governor of California, Reagan is more like a youthful cheerleader, on one side of and detached from the field of battle, rousing his partisan followers to louder cheers for his side. He and his responsive followers are in fact removed from the battle.

Reagan's talent for the simple quip fits neatly into the needs of television news. With occasional excellent exceptions, television normally feeds the audience a sequence of brief items that barely scratch the surface of facts and understanding. The savvy political leader knows that, when he makes a major, lengthy statement on some important public issue, he'll be lucky if it gets twenty seconds of attention on the evening television news. It is common for a Governor to be asked by television newsmen to sum up his views on some vital social issue in thirty seconds. It helps if the politician is negative, if he condemns or attacks, rather than outlining positive and constructive ideas and proposals. His comments then might rate a full minute on television instead of a few seconds. I was always sadly aware that I could command far more attention from television when I denounced an adversary than when I announced the details of some new cooperative program of social progress.

Reagan feeds the voracious appetite of television for the simple, easily understood, negative capsules of news that media executives assume the audience wants. His two-dimensional characteristics keep him prominently on the television screen and help sustain his popularity.

Television accentuates one other problem that is present in any political era. Politicians are human; they err and they have doubts. The people, however, tend to expect political leaders to be free of any confusion; nothing turns them off faster than a candidate or public official who expresses a doubt about himself or his infallibility. Presidential candidate Adlai Stevenson suffered defeats in 1952 and 1956 in part because he admitted publicly, in essence, that he was human, that he occasionally doubted his ability to perform with perfect wisdom and efficiency in the Presidency. Particularly through the medium of television, the people expect a perfectly sure style and speech from their political leaders. The well-modulated, never-stammering voices of newscasters and television performers condition the audience to expect a man to be the epitome of confidence. Reagan comes across on television as totally sure of himself and his views. He rarely stammers, seldom expresses any qualifications or disclaimers to his blunt black-and-white statements and never expresses a real doubt about himself. The appearance of infallibility is misleading and dangerous. Television and Reagan add to a basic public attitude that expects larger-than-life heroes in public office.

The occasional public expression of a doubt does not mean that a politician is indecisive. It is, however, useful in its reminder to the people that their leaders are merely men, perhaps brilliant, potentially great, but always imperfect. The historic truth is that when a people expect to be led by larger-than-life, infallible heroes they usually wind up being dominated by demagogues. I respect the political leader who, even after lengthy study and careful thought, is able to say "I don't know" to some precise question on a tough issue.

Reagan frequently utters those three words, but usually because he has not studied the issue or hasn't even heard of it. He more normally fits the image he often invokes in discussions: the clear-eyed, strong-jawed, Old West sheriff (Warner Brothers version) with an unwavering sense of right and wrong. As a Californian, I want any Governor to acknowledge occasionally the reality of some of the state's problems by admitting doubt about the perfect answer—as long as he remains determined to come up with the *best* answer of which he is capable. As an American, I fully expect any President to have sleepless nights and to reveal doubt in order to give us a sense of his humility; any conscientious man who controls the codes to engage in nuclear war could not possibly be supersure and confident of his wisdom.

Television, however, does provide some immensely helpful influences and services in today's politics. It can expose the patent phony, outright fraud, or clearly malicious public personality. Such men sometimes achieve prominence in politics and can survive for awhile by manipulating the other news media. But television has revealed to the public the excessively harsh or vicious characteristics of such men. The late Senator Joseph McCarthy hit the skids when television gave him intensive coverage during the Army-McCarthy hearings of 1954. California's Max Rafferty, the slickly demagogic Superintendent of Public Instruction, lost the 1968 Senatorial election in part because his offensively belligerent and negative attitudes were observed, via television, by millions of voters. For all the ups and downs of California's politics, most of the state's citizens consider themselves "middle of the road" and are quick to reject the candidate who appears to take extreme positions. Television places extremes in sharp and clear focus, in a way that radio and newspapers cannot.

Richard Nixon was more aware of his need to adapt to

television during his 1962 gubernatorial campaign than during the 1960 Presidential campaign. In the famous Nixon-Kennedy television debates of 1960, he learned—too late—some of the specific, technical problems of his television appearance. In 1962, he undoubtedly realized after his defeat that a radically different and totally new style and manner were necessary for him on television. In the subsequent years and by 1968, he effectively achieved a "new Nixon" image: confident, cool under pressure, occasionally humorous, and avoiding the harsh accusations of "treason" and "Communism" that characterized so many of his earlier campaigns. Nixon has acquired, by hard work and cultivated skill, the mastery of television Reagan enjoys through a more natural talent and his experience as an actor.

One myth about Reagan that is eagerly accepted by his critics is that he is publicly effective only in a controlled, rehearsed situation, as in a motion-picture or television studio, when the script is already prepared and the direction is expert. In fact, Reagan is extremely poised and effective also in the free-flowing give and take of a press conference or any other unrehearsed question-and-answer session. His mind, though confined to simple and rigid dogma, is quick, and there is little hemming or hawing before he offers an answer. He is capable of temperamental outbursts, but rarely loses control while on camera. He seems to employ the old Nixon dictum that a politician should never show anger except when he *intends* to do it for dramatic effect. Reagan seems, and undoubtedly is, relaxed in most unrehearsed television programs or conferences, sustains a tone of almost light banter, and often comes through with a change-of-pace joke to enliven the interest of his audience. Despite his informality, he conveys a sense of strong conviction and sincerity, which is perhaps his greatest asset in the unrehearsed television program. He appears to be calm, confident, and unharried, but also earnest, concerned, and dedicated. I would sum up his style in front of the camera as "cool intensity"—perhaps the perfect quality for a politician in the McLuhan era of communication.

Reagan leaves little doubt that he is constantly aware of the big audience. Most politicians tend to relate—logically and emotionally—to the individual reporter who is asking questions, or a bit more broadly with the newspaper he represents. Reagan relates primarily and continuously with the television audience. As a trained actor, he is able to ignore the clutter of equipment and commotion of reporters at a press conference and keep his eye and a good part of his mind on the audience represented by the small lens of the camera.

The Governor's public comments are often intended to remind the public of his background as a motion picture actor. In his press conference of November 18, 1969, he was asked if he wanted to comment on the news that I was writing this book about his record. Regan responded:

"No, I tell you, I'll wait until I see the picture version, and I'm terribly concerned about who's going to play the title role. If it's Mickey Rooney—he's not tall enough."

(If there were to be a motion picture based on this book, I would insist that Reagan play himself. He's tall enough, but I'm afraid the role would tax his acting talent. In all his years in Hollywood, he never played a villain.)

Any politician faces one perilous temptation in every press conference: to say too much in response to some delicate and difficult question when an extended answer will only dig a deeper hole of controversy or confusion. I admit that this was one of my failings—in terms of political effectiveness— in press conferences; when a difficult, embarrassing, or possibly incriminating question was asked, I sometimes groped or muddled through a lengthy discourse. Reagan resists the temptation. He is cleverly disciplined in ignoring a question he does not wish to answer, no matter how persistent the questioner.

I can admire, and even envy, some of Reagan's talents and skills in the two-dimensional politics of television, but I do not respect his use of them. To me, one of the prime duties and obligations of public office is to help inform the people, to educate them to the facts and meanings of difficult social issues. If a politician does not exert himself in the role of educator, he remains little more than a propagandist. It is the effort to educate the people to the issues and their responsibilities as citizens that marks the politician as a *leader,* in the best sense of that term.

Reagan is not an educator; he is a propagandist for himself and his own narrow viewpoint. He is not a leader; he is an advocate, mirroring and articulating the generally rightwing attitudes of one large segment of society. I believe that, in the complexity of today's issues, a Governor should seek to educate and that, in the crisis of today's polarized society, he should seek to conciliate the contending forces. Reagan not only fails in those functions, he doesn't even try to fulfill them. In today's two-dimensional politics of California, Reagan takes the easy path to political popularity and election success.

The lengthy, logical speech to a live audience is an anachronism in California politics today. Even with expert planning and organization, a politician can hope to reach only a few thousand people in a live situation. The smallest television station in a rural area of California gives the politician an audience of 40,000 or more people. An audience of one million is common for a typical metropolitan television station. This great new channel of communication could be a force for public progress and democratic vitality, but not when the politicians who use it are more concerned about their appearance and the superficial impressions they leave than with giving the people understanding and leadership. Democracy is in trouble if the people are being conditioned to care more about how a man looks than about the realities of his beliefs and actions. I am deeply concerned about a pattern in which the people seem to be influenced most by men who are handsome rather than wise, candidates who are glib rather than informative, and Governors who are expert in creating an impression rather than skilled in the craft of government.

The burden of adding depth and meaning to two-dimensional politics is on the politicians themselves, not primarily on the people or the television newsmen. If politicians offer little more than smiles, quips, and simplistic advocacy, we might as well convert our city halls and capitol buildings into television studios and anticipate the tragic day when democracy will have withered away to leave a vacuum for demagogues to enter.

4

Amateur Governor

In contrast to Richard Nixon's hesitant and unsure manner in the gubernatorial campaign of 1962, Ronald Reagan in 1966 exuded confidence and a cocksure attitude on all issues. One of the reasons for the difference is that Nixon, though unfamiliar with contemporary California circumstances, was experienced and knowledgeable about the workings of government and sensed uncomfortably that he was a stranger to government at the state level. Reagan was completely inexperienced and unfamiliar with government at any level. His simplistic positions on the issues were based on abject ignorance of government, not knowledge or understanding. Unencumbered by an awareness of the legal, administrative, and political complexities of state government, he indulged his ignorance and naïveté with sweeping, unqualified pronouncements during the 1966 campaign.

With a confidence born of ignorance, Reagan equated most of the problems of society with the growth of government. In the campaign, he expressed special contempt for individuals who were skilled and experienced in the craft of government. His basic attitudes were, and are, not only anti-government, but also antiprofessional. He sneered at what he called "professional politicians" and offered the people the superficially appealing vision of leadership by the "Citizen Politician."

It quickly became evident that "Citizen Politician" in reality meant amateur Governor. As Governor, Reagan immediately revealed that he was not only amateurish and ignorant of the basic workings of government but also that he was astonishingly uninformed on the most important issues facing the state.

News reporters were remarkably kind to Reagan as he exposed his continuing ignorance of state affairs in his press conferences during the first year of his term. But the critical reader of the transcripts of those question-and-answer sessions notices an Alice in Wonderland quality to Reagan's remarks. The difference is that Alice, at least, had the curiosity to learn and ask questions as she wandered through a strange realm.

The examples of Reagan's exposed ignorance on important state issues are endless. At times, reporters couldn't believe their ears, but Reagan was unbothered by his ignorance. Early in his administration, Reagan was hopelessly confusing in one press conference on a major financial question until the subject was ended by this exchange:

QUESTION: "Why can't you figure out where the $40 million came from [to pay off a deficit]? You paid the money, but you don't know where it came from?"

REAGAN: "That's right."

In his press conference of March 7, 1967:

QUESTION: "Governor, there's a move in the legislature now to increase the southern California share of the state highway funds from the present 55 per cent to 60 per cent or more. How do you stand on this?"

REAGAN: "Oh, you got one I haven't been into yet. All I know is just dimly that I know there's been this discussion and I haven't looked at it."

In his press conference of March 14, 1967:

QUESTION: "Governor, the legislature is about to adopt a deadline of April 11 for introduction of new bills. Do you think you'll have the rest of your program ready to present to them by that time?"

REAGAN: "Well, I haven't talked since then to my legislative task force on this, so I don't know the state of their preparations. I've often wondered why there are so many laws that have to be passed and maybe we should try to see how many we could do away with. . . . There are only a few more things in keeping with the promises I made during the campaign that I feel a necessity to introduce."

QUESTION: "What are they, Governor?"

REAGAN: "Oh, I'm trying to remember now. . . . I'm going to have to check up on this and find out what still remains."

A month later, on April 11, Reagan still was unsure even about his own legislative plans:

QUESTION: "Are there any of your programs, Governor, that will not be introduced in this session?"

REAGAN: "You know, I honestly can't answer that. We are trying for all of them. I would have to consult with the task force to find out. . . . There may be some things that have to hold over."

Also on April 11:

QUESTION: "Governor, several other Governors have indicated they had been offered a hot line telephone to the White House. Have you been included in that?"

REAGAN: "I think we have . . . a disaster phone. There is a disaster phone connecting Governors. I don't think we can call in. They have to call us. When that one riings, run for the basement. I feel like a little general in Beatle Bailey. Do you think I have been overlooked?"

The lack of details in his knowledge of vital issues was revealed again and again through the years of his term. Dozens of times, reporters caught him with virtually no knowledge of issues that were nearing decision in the legislature or commanding the prime attention of the press and public. Running through his press conferences with startling frequency were such remarks—on *major* issues—as "I haven't thought about that yet" and "I haven't read that report" and "You caught me on that one; I don't know."

Even when caught short on a major, vital issue, Reagan seemed reluctant to inform himself and form judgments. In the spring of 1967, the legislature and the people were giving major attention to a bill to reform California's law regulating and limiting abortions. This was the sequence of Reagan's ignorance and indifference on that issue:

May 2:

QUESTION: "Is there any possibility of a residency requirement in an abortion bill? Would you favor something like that so California wouldn't be 'an abortion center'?"

REAGAN: "I never even thought about that."

May 9:

QUESTION: "Governor, the North Carolina bill has a residency requirement. Is this something you would like to see in a bill California might have?"

REAGAN: "I've never given that any thought. I don't understand. I'd not want to create a kind of attraction in the state for this sort of thing, but I'd never thought about that."

May 16:

QUESTION: "Governor, your own church denomination had a convention here over the weekend and they urged you to support abortion legislation. Has that changed your thinking on it in any way?"

REAGAN: "I'm just as confused as I was last week."

June 13:

QUESTION: "Governor, the Assembly will be voting on this [abortion reform] bill in less than two hours. If they approve it in the form it is in now would you veto it?"

REAGAN: "I've just been asked that question. I haven't had time to really sit down and marshal my thoughts on that."

Even the immense public interest in the abortion reform bill didn't seem to move Reagan out of his indifference. For at least three months, the issue drew heavy mail from citizens to the legislature and to the Governor. That aspect was raised at his June 13 press conference:

QUESTION: "Governor, I understand you received a heavy flux of mail on this subject. Did that have any bearing on your thinking?"

REAGAN: "No, as a matter of fact, I didn't know about the mail. As I said, I've been out of town. I didn't know about the mail until I read it in the paper this morning."

The new Governor often revealed his determined amateurishness by stating that there was no point in his delving deeply into a subject because he was not a trained expert in it. He stated that he would not attend or chair clemency hearings (which I and most other Governors had done) because he was not a lawyer. He was reluctant to read several important reports or meet with delegations on questions about the state mental health program because he was not a physician or psychologist. The attitude was revealed again in his press conference of April 25, 1967, in a discussion on a petition by the Oakland Airport to fill in 875 acres of the San Francisco Bay:

QUESTION: "Generally speaking, how do you feel about the filling?"

REAGAN: "I was afraid you were going to ask that. . . . This is one of those complicated ones regarding conservation. I don't know the answer. I'm not a scientist or engineer. . . ."

Particularly in his first year in office, Reagan seemed to regard experts in government more as convenient buck-passing devices for him to use than as competent professionals on whom he could rely. Many of his appointments indicated a profoundly antiprofessional attitude. He was asked about one questionable appointment in his press conference of March 21, 1967:

QUESTION: "This week you appointed a Dinuba hardware man who was your Tulare County campaign chairman to the post of Chief of the Division of Housing and Community Development. Does this gentleman have any particular background in that field . . . in light of your statements that this administration would find the most qualified persons for the appointive offices?"

REAGAN: "Well, if he didn't have the qualifications he wouldn't have been given the position. And it's just a remarkable coincidence that some of the most capable people also happened to support my campaign."

One of the most dramatic and tragic examples of Reagan's antiprofessionalism was in the field of public health. California, in the years before his Governorship, excelled in that specialized field. In the mid-1960's, the Executive Director of the American Public Health Association, Berwyn F. Mattison, rated the California Public Health Department "one of the leaders in public health work over the past decade or so." Dr. Lester Breslow, the State Director of Public Health, was generally recognized as one of the two or three best pub-

lic health officials in the United States. That judgment was
shared by Dr. Roger O. Egeberg, a Californian and a Republican, who was later appointed Assistant Secretary of
Health, Education, and Welfare by President Nixon.
In effect, Reagan fired Dr. Breslow. The Reagan Administration acknowledged that Breslow was "eminently qualified" as State Director of Public Health, but that the Governor could not retain him because of "basic philosophical
differences." Reagan said of Breslow: "He believes government . . . should play a greater part in certain areas of the
social structure than I. . . ."

Dr. Egeberg was angered by Breslow's dismissal, and other
steps taken by Reagan in the public health field. This is what
the man who became the Nixon Administration's top health
official said in 1968:

"Reagan hasn't appointed [to the State Board of Health]
a single public health expert. . . . The Reagan Administration has an utter lack of a sense of professionalism. It thinks
the government can be run best by amateurs."

Reagan's antiprofessionalism carries over to other fields.
One of his more noteworthy naïve pronouncements came
during a discussion of the need for urban renewal projects
in the slum areas of California's major cities. "The West,"
he said, "was built without any urban renewal program." He
is, of course, alluding to his own view of the Old West, in
which toughness and "horse sense" were among the supreme
virtues. But contemporary California is the antithesis of the
Old West. Some of Reagan's simple, black-and-white pronouncements would have been more suitable to a village
like Rawlins, Wyoming, in the distant and romantic past
than they are to the complex California society of today.
Reagan's "horse sense" isn't going to solve the difficult problems of a changing, diverse society. It takes trained, skilled
professionals to renovate a slum area efficiently or to develop

and administer an effective program to combat tuberculosis. Reagan appears to make two exceptions to his generally antiprofessional attitude. His statements on periodic international crises, such as the *Pueblo* incident, or continuing conflicts, such as Vietnam, indicate that he favors giving immense decision-making power to expert military officers, rather than "amateur" political or diplomatic officials. And, in some areas of governmental authority involving special economic interests, he often gives power to individuals he regards as "experts" but who in fact represent vested interests. To the position of State Real Estate Commissioner, he appointed a former head of the California Real Estate Association who vigorously opposed open housing legislation. To supervise the regulations on the state's savings and loan associations and banks, he appointed an executive of a savings and loan association. He carried this pattern to the point of absurdity in 1969 when he appointed to a scenic roadway board an executive of an outdoor advertising firm specializing in highway billboards.

Reagan's amateurishness verged on the ridiculous in his second month as Governor. He called on all state employees to help fight the cost of government by voluntarily working, without pay, on Lincoln's Birthday, a legal holiday in California. His proposal was insulting, particularly in light of his many campaign statements that denounced the state bureaucracy and left the impression that state employees were more interested in protecting their prerogatives and taking long coffee breaks than in serving the people. But Reagan optimistically predicted that the great majority of state workers would heed his call for voluntary work on the holiday. His grand expectations vanished on the big morning. Reagan was at his desk in the Governor's Office, but, except for members of his personal staff, he was virtually alone in the State Capitol. State offices in Sacramento and throughout California remained embarrassingly empty and quiet on Lincoln's birthday.

Reagan's general solution for society's problems emphasizes such spontaneous, voluntary efforts as the one that fizzled on Lincoln's birthday. When a private, voluntary effort succeeds, he jubilantly exaggerates its impact out of all proportion to reality. After the Watts riots of 1965, H. C. "Chad" McClellan, a southern California industrialist, organized a private effort to reduce unemployment in that Los Angeles black ghetto. He enlisted other industrialists and businessmen to offer jobs for the "hard-core" unemployed, and continued the work during the first years of the Reagan Administration. Reagan was ecstatic in his praise of the McClellan effort and repeatedly held it up as proof that voluntary, private efforts could lick social problems "without a dollar of government funds." McClellan's work was indeed worthy, and he and his business allies did provide thousands of jobs for Watts citizens. But they did not "solve" the unemployment problem in Watts; the unemployment rate in that ghetto was *higher* in 1969 than at the time of the 1965 riots. And McClellan himself scoffed at Reagan's attitude and excessive claims, while noting realistically that both private *and* government programs are necessary to achieve significant progress. He acknowledged in 1968 that unemployment continued high in Watts and told *New York Post* columnist Murray Kempton that he wished Reagan would stop "playing that numbers game" in boasts about the jobs that had been found. Kempton also quoted McClellan as saying that he had found it necessary to fight against Reagan's "reluctance to understand the need for the national government." McClellan added:

"Federal training programs? Hell, our trouble is we don't get enough of them. If we could double the production of the Manpower Defense Training Act skill centers, we could still get every one of them hired. Sure, I give the federal people hell frequently. But I work hand in glove with them, because I know that I have to."

Reagan's unfounded and zealous claims about McClellan's private efforts were meant to bolster his intrinsically anti-government policy. In essence, he wants government to get out of the business of solving social problems and spurring social progress; he believes that private business can do the job. In his view, government is the enemy of the people, the antagonist of their freedom, the destroyer of their liberties, the encroacher on their rights, the thief of their hard-earned money. Even in his inaugural address in January of 1967— an opportunity for the new Governor to offer a positive reminder of the relationship between the people and their government—he was basically negative. He spoke more like a knight chosen to slay the wicked dragon in Sacramento than a man elected to use the structure of government to serve the people:

". . . It is hard to explain those who even today would question the people's capacity for self-rule. Will they answer this? If no one among us is capable of governing himself, then who among us has the capacity to govern someone else? Using the temporary authority granted by the people, an increasing number lately have sought to control the means of production as if this could be done without eventually controlling those who produce. . . .

"Those of us who have been elected to constitutional office or legislative position . . . are of the people, chosen by them to see that no permanent structure of government ever encroaches on freedom or assumes a power beyond that freely granted by the people. We stand between the taxpayer and the tax spender.

"We have come to a crossroad—a time of decision—and the path we follow turns away from the idea that government and those who serve it are omnipotent. . . ."

Reagan expects that businessmen can not only take on and lick most social problems but can also move in on a part-time basis to achieve a pure sort of efficiency and economy in government. But there were few significant reforms or improvements stemming from the innumerable task forces of businessmen that Reagan appointed just before and after his inauguration; about all he could boast about was the saving of $100,000 through a new system of purchasing and using typewriter ribbons in state offices. Many, if not most, of the businessmen he appointed to important state positions left his administration within a year or so to return to private industry. Businessmen simply did not have the time or the interest to flock full-time to Reagan's "Creative Society" banner.

One reason for the reluctance of businessmen to join Reagan's crusade with enthusiasm and sustained effort is that he so tarnished the image of government that they too regarded it as their enemy. Well into his Governorship, Reagan continued to speak of government as if it were an alien force in society, one that should be whittled down in social significance and left with only a few housekeeping chores. I am convinced that Reagan does not just oppose the high costs of government or the cumbersome size and shape of the bureaucracy, but that he considers government itself essentially evil. With such negative perceptions and attitudes, why then should his followers, including many businessmen, dirty their hands in the tasks of government?

Even granting the superficially attractive quality of some of Reagan's rhetoric, there is little basis for respect of his performance in checking the growth of government. There is an immense gap between the vision of his inaugural address and the reality of what he has done in the Governor's office.

On September 21, 1969, he repeated the major theme of his inaugural address when he spoke to a group of California businessmen. "Nothing is more important right now," he said, "than cutting the cost of government. This should be the top priority of every administration. I repeat, nothing is more important than economy in government."

On that same day, Reagan signed into law a bill giving big salary increases to state government executives, including himself. The measure approved by the tight-fisted Reagan (effective January, 1971) boosted the Governor's salary from $44,100 to $49,000 a year, increased the salaries of other state-wide elected officials from $25,000 to $35,000 and jumped the rate for State Legislators from $16,000 to $19,000. In addition, it granted increases of between $4,000 to $10,000 yearly to the many members of the Governor's personal staff. By several reliable accounts, the cost of Governor Reagan's personal office operation approximately *doubled* over what it was during my last administration, as a result of larger staff, plusher office furnishings, and greatly expanded security measures and personnel.

The inconsistencies between Reagan's rhetoric and performance on economy in government would be laughable except for the human consequences. In the same month that he approved the big salary increases for himself and other state executives, he gutted the budget of a program he undoubtedly considered to qualify for his inaugural description of governmental "goodies dreamed up for our supposed betterment." He chopped a $5 million appropriation for the Needy Children's School Lunch Program down to $500,000. State Senator George Moscone, the program's sponsor, noted that half a million school children in California were not then receiving the minimum food requirement for health. Angrily and appropriately, he accused Reagan of "gutless hypocrisy" for the Governor's "tactic to take the heart out of a humanitarian bill he didn't have the courage to veto outright."

There was no move by what Reagan calls the "private

sector" to fill the proven food need of 500,000 hungry school children. His expressions of fond hope that business and industry could solve the obvious problems of society were both naïve and dangerous.

My own attitude toward the role of government in society cannot be appropriately labeled either "liberal" or "conservative," although in times past I freely used the term "liberalism" when it conveyed clear contemporary meaning and connotations. Government, to me, has a significant role to play in achieving social progress, but that role should be limited. Reagan, of course, has assumed that I, most Democrats, and all "liberals" are "bleeding hearts" who are eager to spend recklessly in the name of "omnipotent government." I doubt that he ever even read such general statements of governmental philosophy as these lines from my inaugural address in 1959:

". . . A liberal program must also be a responsible program, a reasonable, rational, realistic program. We must know how much it will cost and where the money is coming from. Benefits will be measured against burdens. A program that pampers the people or threatens our solvency is as irresponsible as the one that ignores a vital need. . . .

"I will recommend an economy-minded budget. . . . I pledge, however, that we will not sacrifice essential services or narrow our vision for California.

"Let us, in our respect and concern for all the people, resolve to prove anew that representative government is the best government."

As I cannot agree with Reagan that government is intrinsically bad, I do not believe that government is inevitably good. I feel strongly that it is as dangerous to expect that government can do everything as to accept Reagan's view that business can do everything. At no time have I joined those naïve liberals who are as excessively optimistic about what government can achieve as Reagan is about what the "private sector" can achieve. A realistic view acknowledges that government cannot and never will guarantee perfect happiness for all citizens. Government can't banish the ills of the world nor can it abolish the imperfections of man. Government can't end sickness and sadness nor can it eliminate entirely the greed, violence, and sins of which man is capable.

But government is an instrument that—in cooperative spirit with business and other private groups—can help to ameliorate the human condition. Respectfully used as a public trust, government can be a positive and creative force of leadership for a better life and society.

During my administrations, many Republicans were often surprised to learn that I did not fit the partisan stereotype of a "liberal Democrat," that I did deeply believe in America's free-enterprise, capitalistic economy, that I shared a respect for most politically "conservative" businessmen, and that I too was against the unchecked growth of government bureaucracy. Some Republicans were plainly amazed also when I called upon business and industry to help government solve the vital problems of society. My method of enlisting the help of business, however, was markedly different from Reagan's. He seems to think that the "horse sense" of the corner grocer, simply because he is a businessman, is more valuable than the expertise of any "beaureaucrat." My attitude was that the most modern, advanced, sophisticated techniques of business and industry could and should be employed by government. In my second term, I ordered original, depth studies of four major social-governmental problems: crime, transportation, waste disposal, and information-gathering. The studies were conducted by private industry, utilizing the immensely successful, interdisciplinary techniques of aerospace "systems engineering," which had achieved rapid breakthroughs in space exploration. Those four studies—unprecedented in government—were completed by such private firms as Space General Corporation. Reagan, the great proponent of business efficiency and creativity, ignored the four valuable reports when he became Governor. Reagan's emphasis is on cutting back government; my emphasis is on *reform* of the structures of representative government. It is obvious today that government is slow in responding to the needs and will of the people. I have concluded that one of the reasons is that there are too many checks and balances built into our governmental system. Some of those checks, designed to protect the people against arbitrary or abusive governmental action, merely stifle initiative and stall governmental action, even when the people clearly want action in some area. It was often evident to me, during eight years in Sacramento, that a clear, urgent, and publicly recognized need could go unmet because of battles between the State Senate and the State Assembly, or between the Governor and the legislature, or betwen the two political parties within the government. The people today provide a sufficient "check" on arbitrary or excessive governmental action, thanks to the immediate and skeptical reporting of government activity by the press and television. If I had any authority today, I would press for substantial reform and reorganization of state government, eliminating some of the now unnecessary checks and balances. Two key steps that I advocate are: A unicameral legislature, to eliminate the continuing and delaying conflicts between two houses of a legislature; and some close approximation of the British Parliamentary system, which integrates the executive and legislative branches of government, to eliminate the continuing, crippling conflicts between the Governor and the legislature.

Other reforms of government are desperately needed, long

overdue and, I admit, difficult to achieve. Government *has* grown too much, but not just in Sacramento, as Reagan believes. In California, as in most states, there are far too many governmental jurisdictions and there is far too little progress toward *regional* governmental authority—especially in the metropolitan areas. California has fifty-eight counties; it does not need fifty-eight counties, with fifty-eight Boards of Supervisors, fifty-eight sheriffs, and fifty-eight different taxing authorities. Los Angeles County has seventy-seven incorporated communities within its boundaries; the result is a huge snarl of conflicting, jealous jurisdictions and an immense hindrance to cooperative, regional progress. Because of the political and parochial jealousies and arguments, it seems a near impossible task to achieve sweeping reform of state government and the establishment of effective regional governments. But today's leaders should commit themselves to the long and difficult effort. If not, government could become impotent.

Reagan fashions himself a reformer, but in fact he has pursued a path of destructiveness of government, not reform. And, in his political naïveté and governmental amateurishness, he has wasted the opportunity to effect change that any Governor—of any philosophy—has.

A new Governor—particularly one who has won election by almost a million votes, as I did in 1958 and Reagan did in 1966—enjoys a tremendous political momentum. He has the respect of the legislature and the most charitable of attitudes possible by the press. For a time—perhaps as long as a year—.a new Governor has the chance to transcend the usual governmental and political conflicts and to establish his own policies and programs. That period of great political potential is usually called a governmental "honeymoon" between a chief executive and the other forces that will later oppose him vigorously.

Reagan muffed the tremendous advantages he enjoyed in

his first year in office. Instead of a "honeymoon," Sacramento languished in a mood resembling a slumber party. For months after the inauguration, the Capitol was in suspense and then confusion about his administration. He was extraordinarily slow in filling major state positions and in outlining major, vital decisions in even the routine operations of the state. Months after he took office, even Republican legislators were plaintively reminding him that a Governor had to *do* things, not just talk about them. I am convinced that Reagan could have pushed through a major and effective tax reform program, for example, during his first year of grace from strident opposition. Instead, he spoke only vaguely about tax reform, presented no detailed proposals, and wasted a precious opportunity for leadership on a vital issue. Three years later, as a result of Reagan's indifferent leadership and political amateurishness, California was still waiting for a significant tax reform program.

The strongest evidence of Reagan's amateurishness—and perhaps the most damaging effects of his naïveté—is in the area of finance and fiscal policy.

In 1967, Reagan faced a specific fiscal problem—the financing of the state's new Medi-Cal program—with a stubborn refusal to employ efficient remedies. Looking back on the confusing problem and controversy over Medi-Cal, the *Long Beach Independent-Press-Telegram* reported on May 20, 1968:

"The Reagan Administration's approach to the problem of financing Medi-Cal can be likened to a man noticing that his couch is smoldering, and then running down the street shouting 'Fire, fire' without even attempting to use his handy fire extinguisher.

"California employs thousands of people highly skilled in the fields of finance and administration. Their experience could have been Ronald Reagan's fire extinguisher. But it wasn't sought or used. . . ."

"If the Governor had sought advice from men experienced and capable in state government . . . he would not have suffered the public embarrassment of having first a Sacramento Superior Court and then the State Supreme Court tell him he was acting illegally [in cutting out Medi-Cal services]. . . .

"The ink used to write the final figures for Medi-Cal in 1967–68 will not be red, but the Governor's face should be."

On the most rudimentary fiscal obligations, Reagan was careless, and, in the view of some Sacramento veterans, he failed in his legal responsibilities. On February 1, 1967, Senator George Miller, Jr., charged that Reagan had failed to meet a major constitutional requirement that a complete and itemized budget be presented to the legislature by January 31. Senator Miller, Chairman of the Joint Legislative Budget Committee and the Senate Finance Committee, said:

"For the first time in my twenty years of legislative service, a budget has been presented to the people of the state with no details of the Governor's plans, with no specific proposals and with nothing but a series of dotted lines saying 'cut here.' "

Senator Miller noted that Reagan's budget "fails utterly in meeting either the letter or spirit of" Article IV, Section 34 of the Constitution, which requires a Governor to submit a "budget containing a complete plan and itemized statement of all proposed expenditures of the State."

The Senator, a Democrat but also a tough fiscal conservative, also challenged Reagan's intemperate charge that my administration had "looted and drained the State Treasury."

"According to Webster, looting means 'illicit gains by public officials.' If we have been looted," Miller asked, "what was taken illicitly and who were the looters? The state's budget is a public record, regularly audited."

After Reagan ran into legal barriers in his attempts for arbitrary 10 per cent cuts in all state programs, a reporter also challenged his "looting" charge against my administration. This was the question and response in the press conference of March 7, 1967:

QUESTION: "Governor, it hasn't been very long since you said the state's financial resources had been drained and looted by the previous administration. Now you're saying that you really haven't been able to find even 10 per cent from that previous administration's budget that you could logically cut. What kind of draining and what kind of looting is that?"

REAGAN: "Well, I'll use the first word, 'draining,' now. . . . We are left with the problem of raising additional revenue to make up that $180 million."

QUESTION: "Shouldn't you have been able to make some very massive cuts in there then? . . ."

REAGAN: "Well, what would you suggest doing without?"

QUESTIONER: "It's not my budget, Governor."

One of Reagan's previous complaints, which accompanied his "looting" charge, was that I had instituted a new accounting system, prevalent among business firms, known as the "accrual method." Reagan called it a "gimmick to hide a financial deficiency." On March 7, he backtracked only as slightly as he had on the general looting charge:

QUESTION: "Are you going to put in a bill for repealing the accrual system?"

REAGAN: "Oh, I haven't even got around to that yet. I think there are certain corrections to be needed in it. There's nothing wrong with the accrual bookkeeping system. . . ."

Reagan's most whopping blunder turned out to be what he called his "drastic step" to balance the State budget in 1967. When all the figures were in, *Sacramento Bee* writer Richard Rodda reported the details and pinpointed the mistake in November, 1969.

"The disclosure that the State Treasury has money to burn . . . verified the prediction of former Governor Brown that the $1 billion tax boost of the Reagan Administration in 1967 was about twice as large as necessary.

"At that time, Brown said that a $500 million tax increase was plenty to solve the state's fiscal crisis.

"But Governor Reagan pushed through a tax program which more than doubled the rates for income taxpayers, boosted the sales tax by 25 per cent, and made other adjustments. This was the largest tax increase in the history of any state in the nation.

"Last Monday, State Controller Houston I. Flournoy announced the state general fund had a surplus of $537 million on June 30, an unheard of amount in state fiscal history."

A few cynical observers suggested that Reagan's Administration had intentionally (and ironically, considering his campaign pledges of 1966) overtaxed the people early to provide the surplus for a tax reduction in the election year of 1970. I doubt that such devious thinking went on within Reagan's offices, and I give him the benefit of the doubt. That leaves only one conclusion: Reagan and his advisers committed a monumental goof in their analysis of California's fiscal situation, to the amount of half a billion dollars.

The people of California paid, and paid dearly, for the amateurishness of their new Governor.

5

The Ax Falls

As Governor, Ronald Reagan has never admitted responsibility for the major errors of his administration. The closest he came to acknowledging a blunder was when he said, with a wry smile, "The best hatchet job they can do on me is in mental health." I am glad to oblige, but no hatchet is needed to expose Reagan's shoddy record of disrupting California's mental health programs. A small flashlight is sufficient.

Just two months after he took office, Reagan abruptly announced an "economy" move to chop apart the state's mental health program, which had been widely recognized as the most efficient, modern, and humane of any state program in the nation. In his fanatic, simplistic approach to economy, a hatchet would have been too delicate an instrument for the new Governor. He picked up a giant ax and swung away at California's mental health programs with about as much precision and compassion as a berserk Paul Bunyan.

Reagan's arbitrary fiscal attack on the state's services for the mentally ill and the mentally retarded was a major part of a broader "economy" crusade. Soon after his inauguration in January, 1967, the Governor announced that he was ordering a flat 10 per cent reduction of the budgets of all state agencies and departments. In mid-March, he grandly boasted that he would eliminate more than 4,000 state jobs within fifteen months. A few days later, one of his staff assistants disclosed that 3,700 of those jobs would come out of the State Department of Mental Hygiene. The drastic cutback of mental health personnel, they said, would save the taxpayers $17.7 million a year.

Reagan used a simple and narrow deduction to justify the huge cut in the Department of Mental Hygiene's budget. In 1959, there were 37,500 patients in California's hospitals for the mentally ill. In 1967, the number had dropped to 22,000. Using all the fiscal sophistication of a grammar school arithmetic primer, Reagan decided that with fewer patients the mental health program could be substantially reduced.

His administration ignored two basic facts relating to the financial needs of California's mental health programs. First, the number of individuals requiring attention and treatment in mental health facilities was continuing to rise, along with California's population. Although the number of institutionalized, full-time patients was decreasing, *admissions* were increasing. Second, the modern techniques and methods that had freed thousands of individuals from full-time institutional care remained expensive; along with everything else in an inflationary economy, the costs of effective treatment were rising.

Reagan's attempts toward drastic reductions of the state's mental health budgets was a tragedy of political callousness toward human suffering. No one will ever know nor can anyone ever measure the harm done to human lives as a result of the Reagan ax-wielding on mental health budgets. As a result of outrage and pressure by mental health professionals, the legislature, and the public, some of the budget cuts ordered by Reagan were later rescinded. But, at the very least, the confusion created by his careless or cynical policies set the California mental health program back several years.

While stubbornly insisting that the significant drop in the number of patients justified his budget cuts, Reagan refused —in partisan pettiness—to acknowledge the progress in mental health programs under my administration from 1959 to 1967. This exchange took place in Reagan's press conference of March 21, 1967:

QUESTION: "Governor, would your statement regarding the strides which had been made during the last eight years . . . be an exception to your severe criticism of the previous administration on nearly every front during the campaign?"

REAGAN: "No. I'll tell you what my criticism was during the campaign. I pointed out repeatedly that the budget has constantly gone up in this area while the number of patients had gone down. And my only mention of this entire program—and I mentioned it several times—was questioning the justification for multimillion dollar increases year after year while the new techniques, the new treatment at home, the use of the modern drugs were reducing the population in the hospitals."

It is useful to report here some of the details of the developing mental health program in California from 1959 to to 1967.

When I became Governor in 1959, I was determined to boost the quantity and quality of the state's services for the mentally ill and the mentally retarded. While serving as State Attorney General for the previous eight years, I had received reports of criminal brutality and inhuman neglect at Camarillo State Hospital. In 1958, I placed two under-cover agents in the hospital as orderlies. Their reports con-firmed, in shocking detail, the extent of the brutal treat-ment of patients and, also, the general inadequacy of staff and personnel. The following year, as Governor, I set the highest priority on reform and improvement of the state mental health program and pledged myself to finding the best possible man to become Director of Mental Hygiene to do the job. A thorough survey convinced me that that man was Dr. Dan Blaine, an outstanding psychiatrist, a tough politician-administrator, and the former executive secretary of the American Psychiatric Association. Blaine was in the East and reluctant at first to move his family to California, but finally agreed—after I had made my first budget decisions as Governor—to take the job.

That first budget called for an additional $6 million to build a new state mental hospital, and the big item seemed essential. In 1959, all of the existing studies revealed that the number of patients in the crowded state hospitals would continue to increase. My predecessor, Goodwin J. Knight, had asked for the $6 million to build another hospital to care for the increasing patient load. Extensive hearings had confirmed the need. I supported and pushed the $6 million appropriation as Dr. Blaine moved his family to California and settled into his new job as Director of Mental Hygiene.

A few weeks later, Dr. Blaine asked to see me for a private meeting. He stepped into the Governor's Office with polite manners and a touch of deference in his voice for the dignity of the place. But he also seemed troubled and ready to fight if he had to.

"Governor," he said bluntly, "I want you to modify your budget. I don't want a new mental hospital. As a matter of fact, there are too many of them now. This $6 million for a new hospital isn't necessary."

I was flabbergasted, and asked Blaine to explain. The conversation went like this:

BLAINE: "Don't give me the $6 million for a new hospital. But I do want $3 million of that for *program*."

BROWN: "What kind of program?"

BLAINE: "I want the money to buy new drugs. I want to make the elderly patients who are mainly suffering physical infirmity comfortable, but also to use new techniques to get them out of the mental hospitals. There are new methods which can cure mental illness more quickly, new drugs which can hasten recovery. I want the money to use them."

BROWN: "But these new things are not fully tested. You may be right, Doctor, but you have limited experience in some aspects of this. I can't take a chance. I've got to make sure we have a place to put the mentally ill."

BLAINE: "You've got to do this. If you won't, I'll quit. I just won't work under conditions which I know are scientifically incorrect."

He left my office with the question momentarily unresolved, but I immediately rechecked some of those who had recommended him to me and contacted other experts in the mental health field throughout the country. In essense, they said that Blaine's plan might be risky but that he and his plan justified the risk. With a touch of anxiety but more with confidence in the professionalism of Blaine and his progressive colleagues, I agreed to the plan.

We did not build the new hospital. Blaine's program worked, dramatically and quickly. Within a few years, thousands of patients who had been regarded as incurably ill were released or on the road to recovery. Lives were being saved. And, in retrospect, it is fair to say that Blaine's program was the best kind of economy in government. In that first year, we did add $3 million to the Mental Hygiene budget to pay for his modern techniques, new drugs, and trained personnel. But we also saved $3 million in that one year by not building the new $6 million hospital, which ultimately was not needed.

Dr. Blaine is an excellent example of the kind of man who is necessary in government today. He was technically and professionally outstanding in the field of mental health. But he also understood the political and educational roles of his position; he effectively fought for the modern programs in which he believed. One day, early in my administration, he came to me with the complaint that a key category of personnel at the state's mental hospitals was inadequate for the task of caring for patients. This was the hospital staff member who, in those days, was commonly called a "bughouser." It was his duty to handle the daily and routine chores of caring for patients who were unable in any way to care for themselves. The job was unpleasant, menial, dirty, and important; it involved, in part, bathing patients, and cleaning the beds and rooms of individuals who had no control at all over the body elimination processes. The "bughousers" had more contact with patients than any other hospital staff personnel. They were paid the meager sum of $275 a month.

Dr. Blaine protested. He asked for more money to train these staff members to give more competent and compassionate care to patients. He fought through an effort to change attitudes toward the position; instead of "bughousers," they would now be called "psychiatric technicians." Dr. Blaine was not just an outstanding psychiatrist dealing with masses of people; he understood the psychology of pride in work—and recognition—for an individual employee. On the basis of solid evidence that the employees of mental hospitals were, in the vast majority, dedicated and conscientious servants of the sick, Dr. Blaine did not seek a blanket dismissal of the "bughousers." He gave them the chance, through on-the-job educational and training courses, to qualify for the title "Psychiatric Technician" and a diploma, which qualified them for higher salaries. I approved his proposals and actions, and the quality of daily care for the mentally ill improved substantially.

Any understanding of the whole field of mental health programs must start with an understanding of the distinction between the mentally ill—who are incapacitated for varying periods because of psychotic disorders—and the mentally retarded—who are more or less permanently incapacitated because of inborn or injury-induced physical defects. To many of us, the most tragically moving condition is mental retardation in children, resulting from congenital defects. Through my years as Attorney General, I was frustrated by an inability to respond to the calls and visits of friends and others who asked my help in getting a mentally retarded child into a state institution. The typical plea went this way: "Mr. Brown, can't you help? There is this poor child who was born wrong. The child is growing now, but will never be able to care for himself, or learn anything in a normal way. This child has to be attended constantly; he can't even feed himself, or dress himself, or go to the bathroom himself. It's tragic enough for the child, but more tragic for the family. The situation is destroying the family—financially, emotionally, and in every other way. This child is clearly an institutional case, requiring constant care and professional treatment. But there's a long waiting list for admission of retarded children to state institutions. Can't you help this child and family?"

As Attorney General, with no official influence beyond my formal duties in law enforcement, I could not help. As Governor, with immense informal influence and with authority over the state budget, I could help.

When I became Governor, I learned that there was indeed a "waiting list" for admission to hospitals for the mentally retarded children of the state. The formal applicants on the waiting list numbered more than 2,000. With the existing facilities already crowded and with less prospect for "recovery" than the mentally ill had, the mentally retarded child and his family faced years of waiting for help, and there was no assurance that the child would ever be admitted for full-time care and treatment. I was eager to exercise my power as Governor to right this wrong. I *knew* that this need could be satisfied only by governmental initiative. It would have been fine—economically and politically—if some private sector of society had been able to care for the mentally retarded children of California. But the cruel fact was that these children were not being cared for properly, and entire families were being destroyed as a result.

I called Dr. Blaine into my office and gave him the order: "I don't care what it costs. I don't care how it's done or what the difficulties are. I want these mentally retarded children to be given proper care, competent care, the care which is necessary to give them some happiness and to free their families for normal lives. In this rich state, I don't want any waiting lists. Whatever it costs, I want to care for these children and save the lives of their families."

Dr. Blaine understood. The priority and urgency was established. We did the job that had to be done, through government and through a budget. Dr. Blaine went to work, and the waiting list was eliminated. Many of the severely retarded children were placed in state hospitals as full-time patients. Some were placed in day-care centers to free their families at least during the working hours. Some were put in the care of private individuals who were licensed and paid by the state. The whole effort cost the state money, but I had no doubt that the lives of the children and their families fully justified the cost.

From 1959 to 1967, the mental health effort was not strictly a state operation, ordered by me and administered by Dr. Blaine and his successor. Through a new law, which I enthusiastically supported, the Short-Doyle Act, the state provided funds to local jurisdictions to boost their services to the mentally ill and the mentally retarded. The Short-Doyle program permitted counties and cities in California to modernize and expand treatment that often required specialized competence for local problems peculiar to the area.

This total effort to expand and modernize mental health services in California through the early and mid-1960's did not attract much attention from the press and public. In a few pages, I now dramatize the breakthrough that pulled California away from the old, custodial approach to the mentally incapacitated and into a new program, which achieved number one ranking from national psychiatric and public health professionals. But the effort was a long, difficult, quiet, and tedious task, which required my commitment, Dr. Blaine's forceful leadership, the skills of professionals in the field, and substantial financial investments by the state.

In early 1967, Reagan's approach to mental health was noisy, confusing, vacillating, amateurish, and based on the most falsely narrow economic viewpoint.

Specifically, Reagan not only ordered a $17.7 million and 3,700 employee reduction in mental health programs. He called for the closing of 14 outpatient psychiatric clinics and the elimination of such special facilities as the Mendocino State Hospital's 400-bed Alcoholism Treatment Center. He ordered the "deactivation" of 80 wards in 10 state hospitals and approved plans to fire hundreds of psychiatric technicians who were receiving in-hospital training to improve their competence. California's mentally incapacitated, I feared, would rapidly return to the care of the "bughousers."

It was clear, in the spring of 1967, that Reagan had not properly studied the state's mental health program needs and had no idea of what he was doing beyond the boastful, arbitrary, and drastic cut in the total program. He insisted that the huge budget cuts and personnel reductions would not lower the quality of patient care—an impossible conclusion even on the basis of common sense.

The new Governor's ignorance of the facts was revealed again and again.

In his press conference of April 4, 1967:

QUESTION: "Governor, you said that you hoped the counties would be able to pick up the cuts. The County Supervisors Association has said they wouldn't be able to pick up those cuts. Do you have any comment on that?"

REAGAN: "I'll wait to see what the individual county supervisors say."

In the same press conference:

QUESTION: "Do the hospitals have discretion under Civil Service? Can they lay off people who are permanent staff?"

REAGAN: "Well, I'm not going to get into the complicated area of all of those rules, because very frankly, I only know there are many of them and I'm not familiar enough with them."

In his press conference of April 11:

QUESTION: "Exactly how will the in-patient treatment of alcoholics be handled to replace the program at Mendocino State Hospital, since there is no other similar treatment available for these patients either on the state or county level?"

REAGAN: "Well, I can't answer that for you right now because there are a lot of details in this that we are still studying."

In his press conference of April 25:

QUESTION: "Governor, on mental health, have you had

a chance to read the Commission report on staff and standards?"

REAGAN: "No, this is in the hands of our Department [of Health and Welfare] now and I haven't."

In his press conference of June 13:

QUESTION: "Isn't it true that for example at Sonoma [State Hospital] there are fewer staff available to treat the patients than there were in January?"

REAGAN: "There may be some fewer. I don't know."

The new Governor and his staff assistants spoke vaguely of a "two-month study" on which he had based his decision for the massive cutback in mental health budget and personnel. When asked to produce copies of the study by members of the legislature, Reagan's assistants refused with the excuse that the study was in the form of "in-house worksheets." Assemblyman Winfield Shoemaker concluded that the absence of any report "indicates why the legislature and the public are suspicious that there may not have been any study at all."

There was other evidence that Reagan had swung his economy ax on mental health programs without any understanding of the facts and consequences. Early in the year, he acknowledged that he had not personally visited any of the state's mental hospitals as Governor. Through the spring and summer, he was repeatedly asked at his press conferences if he planned to visit any of the hospitals. He repeatedly answered that he had no such plans. And, at times, while the whole mental health program was in confusion and thousands of lives hung in the balance, Reagan's attitude was downright breezy. This exchange took place in his press conference of April 25:

QUESTION: "Governor, you say you are going to Los Alamos to see the atomic plant, because you want to get a firsthand look as a Regent [of the University of California].

Yet you don't want to visit, say, a state mental hospital . . . because you don't feel you are qualified in that field. What is the distinction; are you more of a scientist?"

REAGAN: "Well, I think you are trying to compare apples and oranges. Incidentally, speaking of that, I owe the Governor of Pennsylvania a case of oranges. . . . I have not been immune to looking at institutions of that kind. I have been in a number of mental hospitals, not since I've been Governor. The thing that we are dealing with is factual information on the part of these institutions. . . ."

Reagan finally concluded late in the year that he should indeed visit a state mental hospital. In late November, he toured California's largest mental hospital at Camarillo. But that visit seemed far less a fact-finding mission than a staged response to public indignation over his apparent indifference to the human conditions in the hospitals.

Immediately after Reagan's tour at Camarillo, the Union of State Employees charged that it was a "peek-a-boo glance" and that a Hollywood-type setting had been arranged in advance for the Governor's announced visit. The union's officials said that, for the day of Reagan's visit, new clothing was issued to patients, additional shifts of employees were put into duty in the wards, and that bare spots in the lawns surrounding the hospital had been dyed green.

The charges may have been exaggerated, but Reagan's reaction to them was revealing. "Even in-laws sweep the carpet and polish things up when you come for a visit," he said. "That's a matter of pride in your work. Citizens can come through here at any time. There is no special point to my making such visits."

Reagan missed the whole point that the press had been trying to make: that it is difficult for a Governor to gather facts and learn the truth without firsthand, *unannounced* looks at a state program. As State Attorney General for eight

years and Governor for eight years, I learned again and
again that state personnel invariably "spruce up" a facility—
and the truth—when they know in advance that a high
official is coming for a look. It is immensely difficult for any
high public official to acquire a balanced set of facts about
any problem. A Governor tends to become surrounded by
yes-men and sycophants. In response to his inquiries, they
tell him either what they think he wants to hear or what will
make them appear to be successful in his eyes. In his own
office, a Governor must seek to break through the intellectually incestuous relations with his staff and advisers.
To acquire insight or true understanding, he must often
break out of the office itself and get to the scene of a problem.

I did this often as Governor and, earlier, as Attorney
General. During my terms, I visited personally every mental
hospital, every prison, and almost every other state facility
in California. And the key to the success of those visits was
that they were *not* announced in advance. Often, I did not
even plan those visits very much in advance myself. If I was
in some city of the state for a speech or meeting and had
a few spare hours, I would simply decide, on the spot, to
look at the nearby mental hospital. I did not arrive with an
entourage of staff assistants, experts, and television cameras,
nor were the hospital administrators and personnel fore-
warned. On these visits, I did not want a ballyhooed publicity circus; I wanted to see the mental hospitals operating
the way they normally were, without benefit of a "sprucing
up" to impress me. Frequently, I literally slipped into a
mental hospital by the back door, alone or perhaps with
only one aide.

There may be those who consider such conduct sneaky.
But I was the Governor of the state, ultimately responsible
for the effectiveness of state programs and obligated to use

every method I could to inform myself on the realities of state operations. To inform myself on California's mental health programs, I consulted the experts, met frequently with Department of Mental Hygiene administrators, devoured the reports and statistics that came to my desk, and ordered special studies to answer my questions. But particularly for a program of such direct effect on the lives of human beings as mental health, I wanted to see with my own eyes the normal circumstances of the patients and the hospital personnel. With such determination to inform himself and get at the truth, a Governor does not become infallible. But he does make fewer mistakes.

Reagan made a whopping mistake in his attempts to ax California's mental health budgets, in large measure because he did not seek to inform himself of the realities of the state's program. He finally learned and later reversed himself on some of his budget-slashing decisions. But the process of educating the new and amateurish Governor took many months, if not years, and caused immeasurable harm to the state's mental health services. He was a slow learner, primarily because he was at first hung up on his simplistic pledge to cut the costs of government and later because he became uptight about the widespread criticisms of his decisions for mass firings of mental health personnel and deep cuts in program budgets.

When various professional associations and groups of employees in the mental health field began active opposition to Reagan's decisions, he heatedly denounced what he called "blackmailers" and "a high-powered propaganda campaign." At one point he characterized the state's mental hospitals as "hotel operations." A Danish medical official visited a California hospital for the mentally retarded and remarked, "I could not believe my eyes. In our country, we wouldn't treat cattle that way." Reagan reacted by condemning "outsiders," but also ignored suggestions for a study of California hospitals by a team from the Menninger Clinic or even by a group of California experts. When 650 members of the Southern California Psychiatric Society approved a resolution calling the cutbacks "disastrous," Reagan called them "headshrinkers."

As the protests of mental health professionals increased, the beleaguered Governor even spoke ominously of "sabotage" within the program. This question and answer came in his press conference of April 4:

QUESTION: "The Assistant Superintendent of Agnew [State Hospital] has said that under the Civil Service regulations they have to lay off the psychiatric technician trainees because they are probationary employees. When your economy program or freeze [on hiring] is changed they are not going to have anybody to draw on. This is going to have an effect for years to come. What is your comment?"

REAGAN: "Well, my comment is going to sound a little harsh. I don't mean to tell someone else his business, but I'll tell you this: Every time we tried to effect an economy in this state I have found that there are certain individuals directly involved whose only approach to economy seems to be to try and make the cut where it will hurt the most and be the most damaging in order to muster public opinion on their side."

In the midst of the controversy over the mental health slashes, Reagan was often imprudently angry and rude in his reaction to criticism. A few times, however, he responded with a jocular quip, which—to me—was shocking, in light of the human tragedy and seriousness of the situation. These comments came in his press conference of June 13:

QUESTION: "Governor, a spokesman for the Psychiatric Societies of California, Dr. Irving Phillip, says California is not number one regarding the treatment and care of mentally ill."

REAGAN: "This is a technicality. . . . I will challenge him, with regard to the mental health care for the patient, that we are considered throughout the nation to be the leading state. . . ."

QUESTION: "He also says you have to be under great strain personally to [charge] blackmail to the entire medical profession."

REAGAN: "Well, you know, a headshrinker, he's probably sitting there looking at the pupils in my eyes on television. He can see me on a couch now. Well, I want to tell you, if I get on that couch, it will be to take a nap."

That press conference ended with the transcriber's notation: " (Laughter)." The public discussion of the issue had sunk to a ridiculous level, thanks largely to Reagan's intemperate comments.

He also failed to state the truth publicly, on many occasions. In his press conference of March 21—a week after his first announcement of the cutbacks—he was asked about the rate of admissions to state mental hospitals (meaning those who were accepted for treatment) as opposed to the number of patients actually in the hospitals. Reagan stated flatly: "The admission rate has been dropping." This was not true; the admission rate was increasing throughout the state in 1967. At Napa State Hospital, the admission rate was higher than at any time in its history. After he ordered the elimination of fourteen state outpatient clinics, Reagan said confidently that the local, county-operated clinics would handle the new load. But, in September, to offer just one example, the Los Angeles County Board of Supervisors voted unanimously not to take over "after-care" treatment of state mental health patients because the state had not come through with an increase of funds to help do the job.

Reagan could play loose with the facts, denounce his critics, make jokes about the mental health situation, and for a time stick rigidly to his "Nothing is more important than economy" position. But the depth and breadth of the opposition in the state gradually forced him to modify his arbitrary orders and finally to reverse some of them. The protests of professionals in the field became more intense and more pointed. Many of the San Francisco area's private psychiatrists, psychologists, and educators, whose own practices were not in jeopardy, banded together against what they called Reagan's "terrific blow" to the State Mental Hygiene Program. Irving Rosenblatt, Jr., Chairman of the San Francisco Mental Health Advisory Board, said that "the sweet moment of victory [over mental illness] has turned to the sour taste of despair as a result of the mutilation of the California Mental Health Program by the state administration." Dr. J. M. Stubblebine, chief of San Francisco's Community Mental Health Services, said bluntly that, unless Reagan implemented the budget cuts more carefully, "some patients will die." Generally, the mental health specialists argued that a good system and program should not be scuttled just because it had been successful; the need remained. The responsible critics acknowledged that *some* reduction of mental health personnel was possible because of decreasing numbers of full-time patients, but protested Reagan's intention for mass firings with little planning—or funds—for local alternatives to patient care.

As Reagan's careless and insensitive decisions became more obviously dangerous, the opposition was joined even by some of his most steadfast allies. Republican as well as Democratic leaders and members of the legislature spoke out forcefully against Reagan's cutbacks. *The Los Angeles Times*, which had supported Reagan for election and maintained a "conservative" editorial attitude toward government economy, at first (March 16) called his mental health cutbacks "a sensible economy move." By March 30, *The Times* had some second thoughts, saying editorially: "Administration spokesmen may find it difficult to answer the charge of 'false economy' in this strange approach to budget cutting." And by April 11, *The Times* was clearly fearful when it asked for assurances from the Governor "that the drastic cutbacks will not wreck havoc on California's mental health program." After studying the facts, *The Times* also stated in its editorial of April 11:

"It is true, as the Governor says, that the population in mental hospitals is declining. But his own budget document shows that the number of persons treated in such institutions during the year is on the increase. Furthermore, there is a waiting list for admission to hospitals for the mentally retarded, which administration sources estimate at 1,500, but which some sources claim is far higher. . . .

"Furthermore, if reductions in support personnel are found to be based on use of patient labor then these cuts, too, should be restored. Patients' work can be therapeutic, but to use it as a budget-cutting device strikes us as repugnant."

For a time, Reagan ignored the mounting opposition and insisted that patient care would not suffer as a result of his cutbacks. For awhile, he passed the buck to his Director of Mental Hygiene, Dr. James V. Lowry, arguing that Dr. Lowry would work out the details of the cutbacks carefully and with concern for patient care. But Dr. Lowry himself admitted early in the controversy that there were no detailed plans for implementation of the Reagan cuts. (Dr. Lowry, first appointed by me, is a good administrator and a stable civil-service—oriented official; he is not an enthusiast for change, nor is he a fighter, as Dr. Dan Blaine was. Dr. Lowry quietly went along with most of Reagan's policies.)

The evidence and public uproar over Reagan's cutbacks, much of it stemming from thorough legislative hearings on the issue, did slowly and painfully move Reagan. In an early phase of the battle, he agreed to a sixty-day delay in his plans for mass firings of mental health personnel. Through 1967, he grudgingly reversed himself on some of the cutback orders. In 1968, trying to regain some of the loss of popularity on the issue as indicated by opinion polls, he churned out many proposals that would ostensibly improve care of the mentally ill and retarded. By October, 1969, in a speech at Town Hall West, Reagan revealed the full extent of his miraculous public transformation on the issue. Although he began that address (as reprinted in the *Town Hall Journal*) by repeating that "nothing is more important than economizing in government," he proceeded to boast that he had increased the Department of Mental Hygiene budget from $213 million in 1967 to $275 million in 1968!

But Reagan was practically dragged screaming and kicking toward a policy and program on mental health of minimum concern for modern and humane care. It is only mildly comforting that, in our system of politics and government, overwhelming public pressure can convert a Governor of even Reagan's rigid and simplistic viewpoints. But, such "conversions," as in Reagan's case on the issue of mental health, do not have the same continuing impact on public policy as a deeper, personal commitment by the man himself. And the delay of acknowledging and then correcting a major mistake, again as with Reagan and mental health, means months and years of less help and more suffering for thousands of individual human beings.

Even today, I doubt that Reagan's "conversion" on the mental health issue is more than skin deep. I am convinced that his gubernatorial heart still beats to the rhythm of his economy rhetoric, and not to what he calls the "bleeding heart" concern of people who want to do something about human suffering. The fact is that by the beginning of 1970, Reagan had eliminated more than 2,000 employees from

California's mental health programs, many individual services had been terminated and there were growing problems
in the state's mental institutions.

In the summer of 1969, a fourteen-year old boy was homo-
sexually attacked while he was a patient at Napa State
Hospital. There was no hospital employee on duty in the
children's ward at the time of the attack. Reagan's most
forceful reaction to the tragic incident was to condemn the
press for reporting it. The news coverage of the attack, he
said, was "so reprehensible that anyone who has a part in it
should be ashamed of themselves." *The San Francisco Chronicle* commented on the Governor's angry outburst:

"It is, of course, not 'reprehensible' to call attention to
shocking hospital conditions, nor is it an unfair political
attack. The state hospital system, as we have noted earlier,
is sick itself, undermanned and with a surviving staff of
uncertain morale. It is now a system, in many instances,
conducive to neglect, violence, and brutality. The California
public has not only the right to know about these conditions,
and the incidents they spawn, but should know fully of
them."

Fuller knowledge came from a study ordered by the legislature and conducted by the public policy research firm of
Arthur Bolton Associates. Their preliminary report, issued
in January, 1970, declared that the state's mental hospitals
were so poor that they could no longer be considered "appropriate places" for the treatment and care of mentally
disordered children. It declared that treatment was inadequate, crowding in the wards was acute, and living conditions for the children were starkly depressing.

Such reports are valuable, but, even when professionally
conducted and graphically written, they cannot convey significant detail, which can come only from firsthand observation. The Reagan Administration not only denied the basic

contentions of the Bolton report, but the Governor continued to refrain from seeking firsthand observation of conditions in California's mental hospitals.

I will never forget one example of Reagan's callous indifference to those conditions—and his reliance on formal reports—which occurred in the midst of the mental health controversy in 1967. In July of that year, the Governor defended a plan at DeWitt State Hospital, near Auburn, to serve patients only two hot meals a day instead of three. Questioned about the step at his press conference, Reagan said:

"The program they are going to experiment with at DeWitt is an experiment they have been considering quite some time before any talk of economy moves. It is a system that has been put into effect in a number of hospitals through the country."

Reagan had the audacity to suggest that a cutback in the food budget for DeWitt (and other state mental hospitals) would actually result in better and more meals for patients. He referred to "continental breakfasts" and said that the patients would really get four meals a day under the new plan: Rolls, juice, and coffee for breakfast, a hot meal at 11 A.M., another hot meal at 5 P.M., and a snack of sandwiches and milk at 7:30 P.M.

A more accurate and penetrating look at the food situation in state mental hospitals was taken by attorney Paul Berg, a member of the California Association of Mental Health, and James M. Miller, the President of the Sacramento Association for Retarded Children.

Berg surveyed the situation at DeWitt and then said:

"No one can tell me that the quality of food will remain the same when you fire 20 per cent of the cooks. And to say the food will be 'improved' borders on the ridiculous.

"The pitifully low [food] budget of 79 cents per day

[per patient] has been cut by 5 per cent according to a directive sent from the Department of Mental Hygiene to the hospital superintendents April 25, 1967. If the Governor can manage 'improved' nutrition on 20 per cent less staff and 5 per cent fewer dollars for purchase of food, he should be advising every housewife in California how he does it."

The attorney reported that a typical hot meal served to retarded patients at DeWitt State Hospital *before* Reagan's new cutbacks "consisted of ground carrots, ground lima beans, and two and a half ounces of hamburger mixed with oatmeal and water." Berg suggested that Californians should visit the hospital themselves to "view the disastrous results of buget cuts by the Reagan Administration."

His colleague, James Miller, expanded the report. Miller said:

"A 20 per cent reduction in cooks at DeWitt and a 5 per cent decrease in gross food purchase means there are fewer people preparing less food.

"It doesn't matter if they divide that amount of food into three meals, four snacks, or a combination. It is still a decreased amount of food.

"One noon meal served to a ward of children aged six to twelve at a nearby hospital for the retarded consisted of watery navy beans, cole slaw, one thin slice of bologna dry around the edges, one slice of bread, and a cup of milk. Half of them didn't touch it. It was unappetizing, cold, and all run together on one dish. And this was the main, big meal of the day.

"This was one month *before* the 5 per cent cut in food purchase."

6

The Fastest Gun
in the West

Five months after he became Governor, Ronald Reagan
addressed a meeting of the National Sheriffs Association
in Las Vegas, Nevada. He won laughter and applause
quickly, with these opening remarks:

"Las Vegas is really a wonderful place. Where else outside of government do people throw money away? The big
difference, of course, is that here you can do it yourself; in
government, we do it for you.

"But it's nice to see all you sheriffs out there. I've been a
sheriff myself—you can't make a living in Hollywood for
more than twenty-five years without being a sheriff, and if
the picture makes money—polish the star, you'll wear it
often.

"First time I ever played a sheriff, the director told me all
I had to have was a hard head and a white hat. I think your

job takes a little more than that. But I'm sure most of you agree that what is needed more than anything in our country today is people with a hard-headed approach to our problems and a vital interest in seeing them solved.

"This is especially true in the field of law enforcement where the problems increase daily and where there are no easy solutions. I once played a sheriff who thought he could do the job without a gun. I was dead in twenty-seven minutes of a thirty minute show. You may still have your guns, but there are those who've done everything but tie your hands and take your guns. It is time for society to give those on the firing line the weapons they need in the fight against crime. . . ."

In that speech, Reagan proceeded to discuss—with diminishing humor—the basic and urgent problem of crime and violence in America. It was a tough, "hard-headed" speech, which established the basic themes he has repeated throughout his term as Governor.

He laid the blame for increasing crime rates to almost everything from the permissive attitude of parents to the restrictions of child labor laws, with heavy and indignant emphasis on "court decisions which have narrowed the difference between liberty and license." He minimized the factor of poverty as one cause of crime and mocked "the theory that says society is to blame." As Governor, he did not zero in on the villain who had been his prime target in the 1966 campaign: me. And as a former motion picture and television actor, he neglected to mention the screen's glorification of violence as a factor contributing to modern crime.

(In May, 1967, I was struck by the irony of Reagan's reaction to an incident in which a group of Black Panthers stalked into the State Capitol brandishing rifles and revolvers. "Such behavior is absurd," the man who had played so many gun-slinging roles said. "The idea—in a country like ours—that grown men and women think they have got to run around playing cowboys with guns on their belts!")

In his remarks to the Sheriffs Association and in most of his later speeches on crime, Reagan spoke far more vaguely about the *solutions* to the problem of crime than about the causes. "We have four main objectives," he said:

"First, to provide state-wide planning and for orderly and effective development in the field of criminal justice.

"Second, we wish and expect to maintain the traditional partnership and cooperation between the agencies of state and local government.

"Third, we must provide coordination of those agencies and groups involved in criminal justice projects.

"Fourth, we must provide a vehicle to handle federal-state relations, and to implement federal legislation dealing with crime control."

Reagan's "objectives" were a faint echo of his decisive pledges during the 1966 campaign to crack down on crime. "Planning . . . cooperation . . . coordination . . . implementation"? Those are commendable concepts, of course, but imprecise. In a remarkably short time after settling in Sacramento, Reagan was beginning to sound amazingly like the bureaucratic politicians he had for so long denounced. His promised crusade against crime finally amounted to a policy with little substance. It lacked that one vital element that any increased law enforcement effort would require—money. The Governor's economy gospel apparently took priority even over his zealous campaign pledges to reduce crime in California.

Reagan's first legislative program on crime undoubtedly disappointed most of his allies who had expected a great and substantial boost in the state's efforts. It was as spotty as his platform rhetoric was vague. His own 1967 legislative message on crime, in fact, acknowledged that it was designed to strengthen "soft spots" in crime law and prevention. The specifics were meager: a tougher antipornography law, creation of a California Crime Foundation (for "coordination and research"), a "nonpolitical" system for appointment of judges, restoring to the cities and counties "the ability to enact local laws designed to meet local problems," and longer prison terms for certain crimes resulting in bodily harm to the victims. The detail offered with several of the proposals was negligible.

Reaction of Reagan's allies was, at best, lukewarm. *The Los Angeles Times*, though commending the "laudable objectives," complained that "The Governor has not gone far enough. . . . Much more should be forthcoming." *The Times* also recognized the one critical gap between Reagan's promise and performance: "Attention should be given also to the need for additional funds to beef up law enforcement activities."

Even the one, toughly specific anticrime measure by Reagan—longer prison terms for some criminals—seemed a bit shaky in light of his blanket order for budget cuts in all state operations. Two months after he proposed legislation to lengthen prison terms for some crimes, his staff announced that the State Department of Corrections would lose 140 employees as a result of his orders to economize. Significantly, all officials of the state's prisons and other correctional facilities were instructed not to discuss their new budgets with "outsiders."

Aside from the paucity of Reagan's anticrime proposals, his follow-through on his own measures was often inconsistent or contradictory. Generally, I feel that his judicial appointments defied the spirit of his campaign pledges and legislative message. The subject was raised at his press conference of September 5, 1967:

QUESTION: "Governor, so far you have appointed seventeen judges, all Republicans. Now, how does that square with your promise to keep politics out of judicial appointments?"

REAGAN: "Well, it still leaves us outnumbered by Democrat judges three to one. . . . We set up a system, when we couldn't get our Judicial Reform Bill through, voluntarily. . . . We have appointed in every instance only the person that received the top grading, the top total of points, from three separate groups. I don't know what more we can do to try and keep it out of politics than this."

QUESTION: "This produces Republican judges?"

REAGAN: "I have been trying to say that our party, you know, has really got the answers to the problems. . . ."

A second glaring contradiction between Reagan's promise and performance came on the "pre-emption" issue. He had stated repeatedly during the campaign that the state should not "pre-empt" the ability of local governments to adopt local laws relating to crime. His first legislative message urged a measure to establish that principle. But he blithely abandoned the "pre-emption" concept when his right-wing attitudes surged to the surface on one controversial issue: gun control. Reagan opposed steps by San Francisco and Beverly Hills to establish modest, local control over registration of handguns, and he even pushed for state legislation to prohibit cities or counties from adopting such ordinances. The Governor forgot his lofty ideas about "pre-emption" and used language strikingly similar to the propaganda of such groups as the National Rifle Association and the John Birch Society. "People kill people; guns don't kill them," he said. "And a very small percentage, actually, of our crimes of violence are committed with these weapons. . . . I like the idea that the law-abiding can have protection in their homes."

In the gubernatorial campaign of 1966, Reagan placed emphasis on crime and violence as the main election issue. I

do not begrudge the constant attention he gave to that issue
during the summer and fall of 1966. Crime is, indeed, a
pervasive problem in modern society and an important, legitimate subject for public discussion. But Reagan's treatment
of crime as an issue was narrowly political and dangerously
misleading. He spent more time thrashing the already growing public fear about crime and violence than on calm attempts to place the issue in a rational perspective. His outraged remarks about rising crime rates and his hard-headed
demands to crack down on crime matched—and accelerated
—the impatient, fearful mood of most Californians. His
speeches not only dramatized the growing incidence of crime
in California; they sensationalized it. Reagan's receptive
audiences heard innumerable gory and garish descriptions of
crime, which fortified their notions that "law and order"
had broken down and that it was no longer safe to walk the
streets of any city at any hour. In its essential outlines,
Reagan's anticrime campaign in California in 1966 was a
portent of Richard Nixon's (and George Wallace's) Presidential campaign of 1968, with its heavy and graphically
descriptive emphasis on "crime in the streets." Nixon's attacks on the national Democratic administration and the
courts in 1968, on the crime issue, were exact echoes of
Reagan's 1966 attacks on my administration in Sacramento
and court decisions up to that time. In frustration, fear, and
confusion on the issue of crime and violence, the public has
been eager to find scapegoats. Nixon in 1968 and Reagan in
1966 pointed their fingers directly toward the same scapegoats: The courts, particularly the Supreme Court, were
"coddling criminals" through decisions guaranteeing Constitutional rights; Democrats, particularly incumbent Democratic leaders, were "soft on crime."

Reagan's campaign habit of describing particularly lurid
and ghastly crimes in the same breath as he attacked Demo-

crats or the courts continued for awhile after he became Governor. In his June, 1967 speech to the Sheriffs Association, he offered this tidbit:

"Some court decisions . . . have overbalanced the scales of justice so that the rights of society are outweighed by decisions granting new rights to individuals accused of crimes.

"There was the case of the young boy who came home from school and found a man—a boarder in the home—washing blood from his hands in the kitchen sink. He told the boy he had cut himself.

"The boy went into the bedroom where he found his ten-year-old sister's body hidden under clothing and papers.

"He ran screaming from the house.

"The little girl had been stabbed sixty times and had been mutilated in a savage and depraved manner. Cigarettes had been ground out in some of her wounds.

"The murderer was convicted and sentenced to death. But the California Supreme Court in a 4 to 3 decision reversed the conviction and death penalty not because there was any question of his guilt but because of technical reasons and because 'there was insufficient evidence that the defendant intended to commit mayhem or to torture'."

Reagan allowed time for the ghastly details to sink into the minds of his audience, then added—in questionable logic —this comment:

"Obviously, I'm not telling you this with the idea of shocking you with a story of crime and violence. . . . I am telling it only to point up the need for common sense and realism in the war on crime. Let us have an end to the idea that society is responsible for each and every wrongdoer. We must return to a belief in every individual being responsible for his conduct and his misdeeds, with punishment immediate and certain."

As Governor, Reagan's approach to the ancient, complex,

and human problem of crime and violence has been characteristically negative and simplistic. Aside from his occasional statements of vague "objectives" and meager, non-funded legislative programs, he has concentrated on a single solution to crime: tougher punishment for the criminal. In Reagan's narrow view, that means less discretion for the courts and longer prison sentences for the convicted. Swift and harsh punishment, he firmly believes and constantly makes clear, is the prime "deterrent" to crime.

I have always felt that advocacy of severe punishment for crime is the refuge of a demagogue. Today's most expert criminologists admit that they have not found all the answers to the questions of crime prevention, but they basically agree that severe punishment is not the answer. History backs up the modern doubts that harsh punishment deters criminals. One of the more persuasive examples was evident in England a few centuries ago, when convicted pickpockets were put to death in public hangings. The gruesome spectacles were supposed to discourage pickpocketing, British authorities reasoned. But they were disappointed to learn that thieves moved through the crowds in increasing numbers to commit the same crime for which a man was being hung to death a few yards away.

Reagan favors capital punishment as a "deterrent" to crime. I do not, because I do not believe that the death of a man in San Quentin's gas chamber will "deter" other men from committing murder. For most of my adult life, I have been involved in or responsible for law enforcement—as an attorney, as San Francisco's District Attorney for seven years, as California Attorney General—the top state law enforcement officer—for eight years, and as Governor for two terms. I have studied and worked on the problems of crime and law enforcement for most of my life and still know that man and society have not yet found the complete or simple answer to human violence and lawlessness. My continuing doubts that stern punishment provides an effective deterrent to crime does not mean that I am—as Reagan suggested to voters in 1966—"indifferent" or "soft" in my attitudes on crime and public safety. There always will be dangerous individuals in society, those who cannot achieve a moral maturity and who do threaten—repeatedly—the lives and safety of others. This type of individual can be identified by modern authorities and should be isolated from the opportunity to hurt others. I do not regard imprisonment of such individuals as punishment, but rather as a quarantine, to protect other citizens in the same way we protect them when we quarantine a person with tuberculosis or some other infectious disease.

For most convicted criminals, the degree of punishment is a relative thing and ought to be determined, to some extent, on the circumstances of the individual case. Reagan pushed through the legislature and signed into law measures that raised the minimum, mandatory prison sentences for some crimes to five-years-to-life. I doubt that such punishment, applied uniformly to all who are convicted of a particular crime, will deter subsequent commissions of that crime. The personal impact of a criminal sentence varies with each individual. For some men—those alienated from society and incorrigibly contemptuous of all of society's values—twenty years in prison might be shrugged off as "a bad break." For some men, one day in jail might be personally devastating. A wealthy man with an esteemed reputation in his community, for example, is accused of income tax evasion. He goes through what to him is a humiliating process of being fingerprinted, mugged, and identified as an enemy of society. If convicted, he is publicized and marked for life as a felon and deprived of his civil rights and social stature. A single day in jail—along with its attendant humiliations—might be penalty or deterrent enough for many citizens. Twenty years in

prison—or even the prospect of death in the gas chamber—
might not have a sufficient deterrent effect on some of society's more brutal or immature members.

The emphasis Reagan gives to punishment and longer
prison sentences as deterrents to crime is not matched by his
attention to improving California's prison facilities. In early
1970, *The San Francisco Examiner* published a series of arti-
cles reporting on increasing violence and other troubles in
the state's prisons. In reaction to the series, former State Director of Corrections Richard McGee said that the major
state prisons at San Quentin and Folsom were "obsolete"
and definitely "not the answer" to the problem of dealing
with convicted criminals. Roy K. Procunier, Director of Corrections under Reagan, commented:

"For the relatively few serious troublemakers we have no
better answer than bars and walls and strong surveillance.
For the great majority of prisoners, though, we can offer a
measure of hope and a chance for a better life. We try very
hard to do this, even in outdated plants like Quentin and
Folsom. We could do a better job if all prisons were small
and modern, but it would cost an enormous amount of
money."

Reagan, of course, is not willing to back up his policy of
longer prison terms with the money necessary to modernize
the state's prisons.

Reagan's "hard-headed" rhetoric and policy of tougher
punishment have not worked. Crime rates, which have been
rising steadily in the past few decades, shot up sharply in
California in the past few years. In late 1969, State Attorney
General Thomas C. Lynch reported that crimes of violence
—homicide, assault, robbery, and forcible rape—rose more
than 12 per cent in the first half of 1969 over the same period in 1968. Property crimes—burglary, grand theft, and
auto theft—were up 9 per cent. The total adult felony arrests

jumped 23 per cent; arrests of youths under age 18 for major violations were up 20.5 per cent.

In the campaign of 1966, Reagan quoted such statistics and explicitly blamed my administration's "softness on crimes" for the rising rates. Although I am highly critical of his superficial pronouncements and shallow programs to combat crime, I do not now invoke the same partisan judgments he used in 1966. Political leaders and particularly Governors are responsible to do all they can to battle crime, but they do not *cause* crime in our society.

I hesitate even now to use the scary statistics of rising crime rates, because they are, by themselves, misleading and confusing. There is no longer any question that crime, and particularly violent crime, is rising in California and throughout the nation. But public understanding of this urgent problem requires knowledge of some factors behind the statistics.

One major factor that contributes to the rising crime rates is simply that the "crime-prone" portion of our population —boys and young men between the ages of fourteen and twenty-nine—has been growing at a high rate. The baby-boom in the decade following World War II has resulted in an immense increase in that age category today, particularly in California. And 80 per cent of all crimes are committed by males between the ages of fourteen and twenty-nine in the state. Thus, the bulk of the increase in the crime rate reflects the increase of population in that age group.

Crime also rises rapidly as use of illegal drugs becomes more extensive, and our society is clearly in the grip of a crisis relating to use of drugs. Attorney General Lynch's report late in 1969 revealed that adult drug arrests were up nearly 58 per cent over the previous year; juvenile drug arrests jumped 53 per cent over the same period in 1968.

In his efforts to justify his lack of action to fight poverty,

Reagan is fond of quoting partial statistics indicating that crime increased less sharply during the depression than during times of prosperity. But there is no question that poverty, as well as such related factors as high unemployment and deplorable living conditions, does substantially contribute to rising crime rates, particularly when that poverty is concentrated in ghettos in the midst of affluence. The poor individual who is surrounded by and sees nothing but poverty is not as likely to become criminal as the poor individual who sees wealth and prosperity nearby—directly or via television. Expert studies have confirmed that the highest incidence of crime is among those groups in our population whose recent expectations for progress in their lives have been frustrated. The tremendous migration of minority citizens and the rural poor to California in recent decades has been a major factor in California's higher crime rates. They came to the "Golden State" expecting immediate and substantial improvement in their lives. The frustration of those hopes, through racial discrimination and other conditions, led to despair for some and crime for many. Studies of criminal statistics also indicate that crime is particularly high in areas of transient population. The frequent movement of people within California adds to its high crime rate.

Crime is clearly a major problem in our society, and merits the forceful attention of every candidate and public leader. But, as a political issue, crime has become all too often a specter used by demagogic candidates to scare the people into voting against incumbent officials. "Crime in the streets," a phrase connoting grisly dangers lurking at every corner at every hour, became the major, negative catch phrase of Richard Nixon's Presidential campaign in 1968. Reagan expertly pioneered with that same kind of political scare tactic in his gubernatorial campaign of 1966, stimulating public *fear* about crime far in excess of the real danger. It is not surprising that a poll by Louis Harris in the summer of 1968 disclosed that 81 per cent of the people believed that "law and order" had broken down. The attention of the media to increasing incidents of collective violence was one reason, but candidates Reagan and Nixon also contributed to the near panicky fear of the people through their perversion of crime statistics. Both men were fond of quoting such statistical phrases as these, issued by the FBI in 1966: "An American woman is raped every twelve minutes. . . . Someone is robbed every four-and-a-half minutes in this nation."

Such figures need to be placed in proper perspective—something Reagan and Nixon failed to do in their greed for votes. Such perspective is offered in a staff report to the National Commission on the Causes and Prevention of Violence. An article in that 1969 report, by Fred P. Graham, an attorney and *New York Times* legal reporter, concluded:

"By reducing crime to these terms, the 'fear of strangers' syndrome is justified in a way that is not borne out by the risks of everyday life. Statistically, the risk of attack by strangers is one of the least likely hazards that the average person encounters. The risk of death from willful homicide in any given year is about 1 in 20,000, and almost 3 out of 4 murders are committed by family members or friends. The result is that a person's likelihood of being killed in a car crash is almost fifteen times the chances that he will be murdered by a stranger. His risk in any given year of being attacked by a stranger and hurt badly enough to require any degree of hospitalization is about 1 in 4,500—and this is an average possibility; if he lives away from high-crime areas his risk is much lower. As Ramsey Clark [former U.S. Attorney General] used to put it, the average individual's chance of being a victim of a crime of violence is once in 400 years, and Clark always added that if one wished to improve his odds he could avoid his relatives and friends—since they are statistically the most likely to do him harm."

The solution to rising crime rates, I believe, is definitely not found within the fear-evoking rhetoric of the Reagan and Nixon campaigns, nor does it come from Reagan's simplistic demands for tougher punishment for criminals. The *prevention* of crime is a massive challenge, requiring varied steps by society and government to improve the conditions of life for our most impoverished and desperate citizens. The *control* of crime is still a demanding challenge, but the essential need, I feel, is relatively obvious: more police and more modern police methods. To reduce the soaring crime rates, governments must move to place more policemen in the high-crime neighborhoods of our cities and communities. And they must move to improve the *quality* of police departments. That means higher salaries for policemen, better communications equipment, and more sophisticated training and techniques in crime control. Such steps require leadership at the highest political levels—and money. Reagan has provided neither; he has been content to offer the people only an angry, louder echo of their fears.

It is interesting that not even Reagan could complain in his campaign statements about organized crime of the syndicate variety in California. The reason is that organized crime —as opposed to crime by the individual entrepreneur—has never been able to get a toe hold in California. The only way in which organized crime can flourish is through an alliance between syndicates and local public officials to tolerate illegal gambling, abortions, prostitution, drug sales, and extortion. No such alliances have developed in California, because law enforcement officials in this state have been overwhelmingly honest and incorruptible. There were times when I disagreed with some of the social attitudes of such men as Chief William Parker of Los Angeles and Chief Thomas Cahill of San Francisco, but those top lawmen in the state's two biggest cities—and the chiefs of California's other major cities—were honorable and honest in their police work. In recent decades, California has also elected dedicated Attorneys General—myself, Stanley Mosk, and Thomas Lynch. We were criticized often for some of our policies or programs, but no one—not even Reagan—could accuse us of being in cahoots with the Mafia or any other syndicate-family–type mob.

Once the 1966 campaign was over and Reagan no longer felt compelled to continue his "soft on crime" charges against me and other Democratic officials, he played a different tune. A few weeks after he became Governor, he told a gathering of the state's law officers that "California is fortunate to have the best law enforcement to be found anywhere in the world."

As Governor, Reagan has however continued to damn and denounce the courts with almost as much fervor as expressed by Alabama's George Wallace. There is an ironic contradiction apparent in Reagan's "law and order" attitudes, which was noted in a reporter's question during a 1968 press conference:

QUESTION: "Governor, . . . during the past year you've been highly critical of some of the statements of the courts, including the California Supreme Court, which you consider to be beyond the boundary of propriety. At the same time you condemn—rather, refuted those who choose to disobey laws that they find immoral. Is there some inconsistency here? Some people have criticized you as the person who wants to uphold law for others, but who will readily dissent from a court decision if it goes against you."

REAGAN: "No, as a matter of fact, I've never advocated dissenting from a Court or not upholding a court opinion. . . ."

The Governor added in that answer that he had a right to "criticize" court decisions. But he neglected to mention the vitriolic tone of so many statements in which he had impugned the integrity of respected judges and justices. Frequently, Reagan angrily denounced the courts and specific court decisions almost in the same breath as he complained that public respect for the law was breaking down. In early 1970, a Los Angeles judge completed an exhaustive legal study of school segregation in the area and issued a lengthy, carefully written decision ordering school integration there on constitutional grounds. Reagan, hotly contentious in the midst of a controversy over the school busing issue, condemned that judge's decision as "ridiculous."

Reagan's angry and open denunciations of the courts have followed judicial decisions in a variety of areas from school integration to state medical care for the elderly. Most often, his wrath has been aroused by court decisions protecting the constitutional rights of individuals accused of or arrested for crime. His phrasing in such denouncements usually leaves the impression that he believes the courts are in some sort of conspiratorial alliance with the criminal elements of society, not only condoning but encouraging crime. It is another irony of the Reagan record that he, like so many right-wing conservatives, is constantly lauding the United States Constitution as a brilliant document of law but also constantly denouncing the specific application of the Bill of Rights and other provisions of the Constitution to protect contemporary citizens from the abuses of authority.

In the area of civil liberties—rights of the individual guaranteed by the Constitution—Reagan's attitudes seem to stem from the values of the Middle Ages and the mood of the Old West. One example of the Governor's basic approach to civil liberties will suffice. In March, 1970, a United Press International reporter from Los Angeles was arrested in Santa Barbara while he was officially covering student disturbances near the University of California campus there. The reporter, Stewart Slavin, showed police his valid press credentials, but he was handcuffed and then jailed for twenty hours and told that he was charged with "curfew violation" and that bail would be $1,250. During the twenty hours, he was denied permission to make a phone call to his office, family, or legal counsel. Slavin was later released and the charge was dropped, but UPI President Mims Thomason protested in a letter to Reagan "the utter disregard shown by law enforcement authorities in Santa Barbara . . . to the professional and personal rights of a United Press International correspondent." When Reagan was asked to comment on the violation of the reporter's civil liberties, he responded, "He should be happy he was captured by the good guys."

In his simplistic and angry statements on crime and lawlessness, Reagan's greatest disservice to the people of California has been to blur the distinctions between the hardcore, incorrigible criminal and the amateur, one-time law violator; between individual crimes of violence and collective civil disobedience or, even, peaceful demonstrations. The people need to be aware of those distinctions and to understand the different causes and types of crime and turmoil in our changing society. Reagan, however, obscures the differences and diminishes understanding by his blanket indictment of almost any form of crime, disorder, and staged dissent as "lawlessness on the streets." He occasionally offers parenthetical qualifications to his categorical statements on "lawlessness," but the total effect of Reagan's rhetoric is to accelerate the fear by citizens of "the bad guys." To Reagan and his fearful listeners, "the bad guys" include not only the individual rapists and robbers who lurk with knives in the dark of city streets, but also whole groups of a restless population that take to the streets: Black Panthers and civil rights marchers, student radicals and youthful demonstrators, draft resisters and antiwar protesters. To Reagan and those who swallow his impatient rhetoric, the turbulence of modern society is reduced intellectually to the simplicity of one of the villages built for Reagan's innumerable Old West motion pictures. It's the hard-headed, white-hatted, tough-talking, pure-hearted sheriff against "them"—a broad grouping of not only those who break the law but also those who threaten custom. Reagan capitalizes politically on the natural fear that human beings feel toward the "stranger in town." He cultivates, for votes, the anxiety of those Californians who feel threatened by those they do not know or understand—which often means blacks and long-haired youths who are challenging the status quo with increasingly strident voices. "Polarization" is too mild a term for what is happening in today's society; the pattern is more like a fragmentation of social forces, at war with each other. Reagan's warlike stance on so many issues and toward so many groups of Californians accelerates the polarizing process, which undermines public acceptance of diversity within society and threatens the disintegration of democracy itself.

Reagan speaks often about the nobility of "freedom" and "liberty," but I doubt that he has any pragmatic conception of those worthy human conditions in today's complex society. The best answer to the Reagan mentality in today's politics—and the best warning to a fearful and confused society—is summed up by this favorite quote of mine from George Bernard Shaw:

"It is quite useless to declare that all men are born free if you deny that they are born good. Guarantee a man's goodness and his liberty will take care of itself. To guarantee his freedom on condition that you approve his moral character is formally to abolish all freedom whatsoever, as every man's liberty is at the mercy of a moral indictment which any fool can trump up against everyone who violates custom, whether as a prophet or a rascal. This is the lesson democracy has to learn before it can become anything but the most oppressive of all the priesthoods."

7

A Black and White Issue

In recent years, much of the public discussion about racial problems in our society has been hypocritical. Most of those who have opposed school integration—and the busing of children into different neighborhoods to achieve it—have cited the high costs of such efforts. Opponents of measures to ban discrimination in housing have debated the legal nuances of the Constitution. Fair-employment practices have been opposed with sophisticated, statistical evidence relating to the expense of job-training programs. Innumerable other civil rights proposals have been countered with such neatly rational maxims as "you can't legislate changes in human nature" or intellectual discourses on the relationships between federal authority, states rights, and individual liberty.

The movement toward racial equality and harmony has been complicated by all those arguments. But the basic factor that has thwarted progress and led to tensions and violence is emotional. To be blunt: Most white Americans do not know or understand the Negro and do not like their stereotype of him. And most blacks do not trust the white American and resent him.

For a full decade ending in the mid-1960's, the nation prided itself on the legislative and economic "breakthrough" of racial barriers. California liberals in particular were smugly pleased by the new pressures against segregation in such far-off places as Alabama and Mississippi and righteously assumed that their state was free of any widespread discrimination.

The illusion was abruptly shattered in 1964, when the state's voters rejected, by a two-to-one margin, a new law banning racial discrimination in the sale or rental of housing.

The self-satisfied attitude was violently shattered in 1965, when the black ghetto of Watts in Los Angeles erupted into riots that left thirty-four dead and whole neighborhoods in flames.

The lingering presumptions of innocence by many northern Californians were shattered in 1966, when the black ghetto of San Francisco's Hunter's Point area was torn apart by similar riots.

The so-called "white backlash" to black militancy and rage came earlier to California than to the rest of the nation. I always considered the phrase itself a misnomer. What happened first in California and later nationally was not so much a backlash reaction to black action as it was a surfacing of deep white antagonisms toward the Negro—antagonisms sometimes based on fear, sometimes related to guilt. For years, I had noticed the discrepancy between the expressed morality of "tolerance" and the slightly submerged emotion of repulsion that many white Americans felt toward blacks. In frequent conversations with individuals, I heard the nice intellectual statements about "equality," but then, after a few drinks or in a sudden flash of candor, my companions would blurt out such comments as "I just don't want some noisy Negro family living next door to me" or "It makes me uncomfortable to think of my daugher dating a black boy."

As a politician and then as Governor, I remained aware of the incipient prejudice of many whites and the increasingly volatile moods of blacks and tried to achieve some progress. A strong Fair Employment Practices Act was established in California during my first term. I campaigned for open housing and other civil rights measures and tried to increase my own contact and rapport with the citizens of black and Mexican-American communities in the state. For a time, my approach to racial equality not only satisfied a need to translate my convictions into action but was also politically respectable. In the late 1950's and early 1960's, civil rights advocacy in California was, at least on the surface, stylishly "in."

But in the mid-1960's—and particularly after the voters rejected the Rumford Open Housing Act—progressive political leaders were challenged by an apparent turn toward racial bias by a majority of Californians. Some politicians were confused and brooded about how they could now "handle" the civil rights issue. Even before the Watts riots, many politicians were beginning to muffle their previous civil rights views. The reports by public opinion pollsters bolstered the strategy of caution by pragmatic politicians. The polls disclosed, in late 1964 and early 1965, that a growing majority of Californians believed that the Negro was "moving too fast," that civil rights demonstrations were one step removed from violence in the streets, and that Negro and other minority citizens should turn off the pressure and instead work to "consolidate" their recent gains.

Soon after the Watts riots in August, 1965, I realized the

full depth and intensity of racial antagonisms in California. On one walk through Watts in an attempt to learn more about the reasons for the riots, only a few blacks would speak to me at all, and then in short, cryptic pronouncements:

"After awhile, you just get tired of kicking the wall."

"Man, have you seen *Newsweek* and *Life*. I mean we are on the covers. They know where Watts is now."

"Whitey, we just don't need you any more."

A few hours later, in a downtown hotel just a few miles away from Watts, I listened to the comments of several white community leaders:

"I'm the first to understand what discrimination means, mind you, but that's no cause for rioting and looting."

"I'm just as liberal on the Negro struggle as ever, but frankly, I'm getting fed up with all this violence."

"It's time to get tough with those people. They've got to respect law and order."

". . . law and order . . ."

". . . law and order . . ."

". . . law and order . . ."

A month later, I mingled with the guests at a cocktail party in a pleasaont northern California suburb several hundred miles away from Watts. I winced at the progressively more angry comments about Watts by individuals who regarded themselves as "liberal":

"Terrible, just terrible, those riots. I can't believe it. Why, I drove through Watts once. There aren't any tenements there. Lots of nice little bungalows and gardens."

"Something's got to be done about those people."

"We've coddled them long enough."

"There's talk about those people rioting here. We've got to make sure we're safe."

"I bought a Smith & Wesson, .38 caliber."

"Mine is a dear little pearl-handled thing; fits right into my purse."

"You know what I'd do if I were Chief? I'd shoot them, just line them up and shoot them at the first hint of trouble. That'd stop them."

I knew that some of the comments were uttered in the anguish and confusion of the weeks immediately following the shock of the Watts riots. But I also perceived a deeper and more intransigent attitude developing among whites on one side and blacks on the other. I worried for my state and nation and, more selfishly, about my prospects for re-election as Governor.

In the gubernatorial campaign of 1966, I forcefully condemned rioting and violence and stood by a policy of using law enforcement personnel and the National Guard whenever necessary to prevent or put down violence. I undoubtedly matched Ronald Reagan's use of the popular phrase "law and order," but I also understood that that three-word phrase by itself was becoming to many voters a euphemism for harsh, hard-headed repression. Reagan's campaign emphasized "law and order"—period. Against the advice of my more pragmatic political advisers, I also spoke of the need for "justice—compassion—understanding" and the continuing challenge to eliminate the conditions of discrimination and poverty, which fed the violence. Those were not popular words and concepts in the ugly racial moods of California in 1966. Republican charges that I was "soft" or "vacillating" about violence were a contributing factor to my defeat. In November, I won the votes of black and Mexican-American communities by majorities as high as 90 per cent. Statewide, Reagan beat me by almost a million votes.

It would not have been possible for me to cater in any way to the white backlash that was present in 1966, to win more of the majority vote. My attitudes on racial and religious discrimination were deeply ingrained in me early in my life. It's difficult to define the reasons for such values, but I do credit my mother. She conditioned me as a child to know that no man is better, or worse, than another man because of his religious beliefs or racial background. My father was a Catholic, but my mother, a Unitarian, had an open attitude toward diverse religious viewpoints. She took me to a variety of religious services: Presbyterian and other Protestant churches and several synagogues. Religious and racial tolerance was drilled into me by my mother, and my attitudes were set firmly by the time I was in high school. After my election as Yell Leader—a prestige position—in high school in my junior year, I was invited to join both of the school fraternities. I was interested, but asked that a friend of mine, a Jew, be accepted with me. Fraternity spokesmen turned him down because he was a Jew. I didn't hesitate then to decline their invitation. We ignored the two existing fraternities and organized our own, completely free of any religious or racial discrimination.

Reagan has stated repeatedly—and I believe him—that he personally opposes racial discrimination and is devoid of racial prejudice. My criticism is that, as Governor, he has failed to recognize and deal with this problem, which remains the most urgent and divisive in our society. I doubt that he understands sufficiently the frustrated yearnings of blacks, Mexican-Americans and other minorities. I know that he has failed to exert the calm, compassionate, and forceful leadership that our society's racial crisis so desperately needs. At the national level, Richard Nixon seems to adopt a strategy of ignoring the racial crisis and rationalizing his indifference with Daniel P. Moynihan's patronizing concept of "benign neglect." Reagan's words and deeds are worse. His simplistic "good guys—bad guys" attitudes, revealed often in his reactions to racial turmoil, accelerate the ugly movement toward racial war.

Reagan's basic attitudes were indicated early in his term. For the inaugural ceremonies, he broke a long tradition calling for the Chief Justice of the State Supreme Court to administer the oath of office. Instead, he picked Associate Justice Marshall Francis McComb, best-known throughout the state for his personal and judicial opposition to the Rumford Fair Housing Act. Soon after he became Governor, Reagan angered a group of Negro legislators who met with him in his office. They reported that he regarded the fair housing law as a form of fascism, and quoted him as saying: "You wouldn't want to sell your house to a red-headed Kiwanian if you didn't want to, would you?"

In his press conference of July 25, 1967, Reagan showed a typical lack of restraint in discussing the volatile situation in black ghettos and also revealed the superficiality of his methods to learn something from Negroes themselves. While riots were erupting in Detroit and other cities, this exchange took place between Reagan and newsmen:

QUESTION: "The current situation in Detroit—has it caused any change in your thinking on possible riot controls in the state?"

REAGAN: "No. We are continuing to work with local authorities, and keeping in touch. . . . I had an opportunity to speak the other day to Chief [Thomas] Cahill of San Francisco on this very subject. He assured me that they are aware of the possibilities, that they are planning. So this is about all we can do."

QUESTION: "What do you think of this plan in Sacramento of having members of minority communities form block controls to more or less hold the line before any violence starts?"

REAGAN: "I think it is a great idea. I think the time has come to recognize—and it is very apparent in Detroit right now—that these are no longer riots connected with civil rights in any way. These are riots of the lawbreakers and the mad dogs against the people. The first victims . . . are the good, responsible members of the Negro community. . . . The white and the Negro community have a great deal in common with regard to opposing these mad dogs who are creating this kind of violence. . . ."

QUESTION: "You met with several of whom you called 'responsible Negro leaders.' Later on Senator [Mervin] Dymally and other Negro leaders complained . . . that you really did not meet with the men and women who have a following and an influence on the streets of the Negro communities. What is your reaction? . . ."

REAGAN: "Well, it depends on the kind of following he is talking about. If he means am I going to have a meeting with Stokely Carmichael, no. . . . Senator Dymally's criticism was unwarranted. . . . We had a good meeting. . . . These were what could be called responsible, leading citizens in their various professions and communities. . . ."

QUESTION: "Assemblyman Willie Brown added a little bit to that charge about the Negroes that you met with last week. He said that all but one of them were Republicans and that they also had some connection with your '66 campaign."

REAGAN: "How else could I get acquainted with them? This is true. It may come as a shock to Willie Brown to discover I am a Republican, but I don't think there was anything wrong with being with the leadership of my own party, and that's what they were."

The Governor continued to insist that turmoil in black ghettos was the work of a miniscule percentage of Negroes whom he labeled "mad dogs," and he remained ignorant of the pattern of discontent and anger spreading through black communities. He also wrote off the cause of the riots as stemming from some sort of conspiracy, but couldn't back up that view with any facts, as in this exchange in his July 25 press conference:

QUESTION: "Do you think these riots are being set up on some kind of a nationally organized basis?"

REAGAN: "I think it would be pretty naïve to think these riots are just spontaneous. We have read statements in your own papers that authorities have identified in each riot . . . the presence of the same individuals who seem to be traveling a circuit. I just don't believe these are spontaneous uprisings. I think there is a plan. . . ."

QUESTION: "If there is a plan, will you elaborate to some extent on whom you believe is doing the planning?"

REAGAN: "What?"

QUESTION: "Will you elaborate on who you think is doing the planning if, as you say, there is a plan?"

REAGAN: "No. You would have me guessing then and you would have me trying to name names and establish guilt or innocence on the part of individuals, and I am not an investigating agency. I don't have access to that information."

QUESTION: "How do you know there is a plan then?"

REAGAN: "I said there is the appearance, and I think it would be pretty naïve not to believe it. . . ."

There is no doubt that some black militants do seek to foment and even organize violent activities. But it is naïve— and dangerously misleading—for Reagan to state that black violence stemmed primarily from a few "mad dogs" and conspirators. The race crisis is obviously more profound than that and cannot be resolved until the public leaders and the people understand its varied causes.

America today is confronted by the natural consequences of two centuries of suppression of the Negro. One inevitable consequence was the emergence of such groups as the Black Panthers, organized first in California in the 1960's. As younger blacks mastered their fears, they became more militantly impatient with the continuing injustices of white Americans, and many were attracted to the activist Panthers. Finally, unafraid and proud, they realized that years of passive subservience had to be replaced by organized, tightly disciplined "self-defense." I can partially understand why the Black Panthers gained some momentum among young blacks for its advocacy of violence as a tactic. But I cannot condone a form of militancy based on the threatening use of guns and violence. As a young District Attorney in San Francisco, I saw the victims of guns and developed a horror for violence in any form. I learned that organized violence inevitably results in repressive measures, against not only minority groups but, more subtly, the majority of citizens as well. Tragically, the Black Panthers' use of guns and threats of violence have resulted in systematic repression across the nation. Police and other law enforcement authorities have, in fear, overreacted to the Panthers. Brutal and unconstitutional police tactics have too often increased the appeal of the Panthers, by cloaking them with martyrdom, and have added to the general fear of racial repression among all Negroes.

Reagan's naïveté and shallow knowledge of the racial crisis were indicated in this brief exchange at another press conference in July, 1967:

QUESTION: "Governor, how would you assess the state of race relations in California at the present time—good, bad, explosive, or what?"

REAGAN: "Well, I know that from both communities—the majority and the minority communities—there are a great many hopeful signs and programs working, programs involving some of our fine athletes on playgrounds in the summer, and I think that this kind of bridging must pay off eventually. . . ."

In California, Reagan occasionally acknowledged "legitimate grievances" among blacks. Outside the state, however, he seemed more ambivalent.

In September, 1967, Reagan was, to put it most kindly,

lukewarm about civil rights legislation, when he spoke at a Republican fund-raising dinner in Columbia, South Carolina:

"Everybody is entitled to equal rights, and it is the obligation of the federal government to enforce those rights. Maybe, in some cases, though, the problem is solved for some at the expense of taking away the constitutional rights of others.

"It doesn't do good to open doors for someone who doesn't have the price to get in. If he has the price, he may not need the laws.

"There is no law saying the Negro has to live in Harlem or Watts."

His vacillation on the issues of segregation and discrimination was apparent again at the National Governors Conference in Cincinnati, Ohio, in July, 1968. At that conference, Michigan's George A. Romney introduced a resolution, which called for determined efforts "to maintain law and order with justice; eradicate racial discrimination in employment, in labor unions, and management practices, in the purchase, sale, and rentals of real estate, in the education of children, and in social services." Reagan was the *only* Northern Governor voting against the Romney resolution. When the resolution was approved—with only four other negative votes, all of them cast by Southern Governors—Reagan hustled to withdraw his negative vote to "abstain." He said he objected to a section of the resolution calling for an end to discrimination "by state, local, and private initiative where possible and by Federal action if necessary." He also told reporters later that he had not "thought fast enough" to abstain when the vote was first taken. That, I am convinced, was one of the least impressive displays of political fence-straddling in American history.

Reagan also seemed to have mixed feelings about the exhaustive study and excellent report by the National Advisory Commission on Civil Disorders, released in early 1968. On March 5, he was asked about the report:

QUESTION: "Governor, the President's Commission takes a rather grim view of the situation between the races in this country and the future. . . . Do you share this rather pessimistic viewpoint of the commission and how do you size up the relations between the races in the United States today?"

REAGAN: "Well, I disagree with the report in that regard. I think that it failed to recognize the efforts that have been made by millions of right-thinking people in this country of all ethnic backgrounds and all racial backgrounds who have been trying and making progress. . . ."

QUESTION: "Are you quibbling then, Governor, with the conclusion that the white race is to blame in part for the riots?"

REAGAN: "Well, there is no question that prejudice is going to bring about animosity. . . . To speak only of the root causes, to ignore the fact that there are people who are agitating for disorder and riot . . . is to be pretty naïve about the Stokely Carmichaels and the Rap Browns who are traveling from state to state, city to city, inciting to riot and disorder."

Apparently—and typically—Reagan didn't bother to read the riot commission report, one of the most thorough and insightful studies of a social crisis ever published. The report did give substantial attention to the efforts of black militants to stimulate black protest and violence. The *Sacramento Bee*'s comments on Reagan's criticism of the report were appropriate:

"Gov. Ronald Reagan supplied the typical knee-jerk reaction of the conservative to the report. . . .

"If only things were as simple as Reagan would have the public believe, all the nation would have to do would be to imprison a few militant Negro leaders and all would be well.

"Reagan's thinking on social problems seems to be lobotomized toward an invincibly simplistic approach. . . ."

The Governor also suggested that his administration was "already going a long way" in implementing the recommendations of the riot commission report to eliminate the "root causes" of black unrest and violence. "The answer," he said, "is to jobs, to equal opportunity, to better ways of living and better housing and better education. These are the things that we should be doing. . . ."

Reagan's deeds—and his inaction—mocked his words. On the "root causes" of poverty, unemployment, discrimination, and unequal opportunities, Reagan's efforts throughout his term as Governor have been at best negligible. He has consistently opposed or cut back budgets for low-cost housing programs. He has slashed the appropriations for job-training programs. He has vigorously and constantly axed state funds for education, including the modest sums earmarked by the legislature for schools in ghetto areas. He has steadily condemned federal antipoverty programs, and even boasted that he vetoed, as Governor, more federal antipoverty grants to California than any other Governor, including Wallace of Alabama. He has closed down a score of service centers in the state, which were providing help to the minority poor in job placement, training, and other opportunities. He has mocked the federal "War on Poverty" effort and launched his own "war on welfare" crusade, indiscriminately chopping welfare budgets and exaggerating the incidence of "fraud" among welfare recipients. He fought to scuttle the state's "Medi-Cal" program, of benefit primarily to the elderly and the minorities, and denounced the legislature and the courts when they kept that program intact. He has been a steadfast opponent of concrete steps toward school integration and has continually opposed the Rumford Act, California's fair housing law.

Reagan has reserved special contempt for federal efforts to

reduce or eliminate the "root causes" of discrimination and poverty. His views remained so rigid that he seldom felt any need to give more than cursory attention to federal legislation in the field. His ill-informed attitude was revealed in this exchange in his press conference of March 12, 1968:

QUESTION: "Governor, yesterday the Senate passed on a 71 to 20 vote an open housing statute. Can you tell us whether or not you support that statute?"

REAGAN: "The Senate in Washington?"

QUESTIONER: "Yes."

REAGAN: "I haven't seen it or been able to read the Civil Rights bill that was passed out. Certainly it must have some merits. . . . Our two California Senators voted for it. . . . My main point is I've never changed my opinion and haven't changed it now, about the inability to solve some things with legislation or with law. The main problem must be solved by people, by right-thinking people. . . . I think we have placed too much faith in trying to legislate morality by law and not enough in using the leadership of the people to bring about the voluntary changes that must be made. . . ."

QUESTION: "Governor, Assemblyman [William] Bagley today issued a press release urging you to support the federal open housing law that just passed the Senate, to push it through the rest of the Congress. What is your answer going to be to him?"

REAGAN: "Well, I think the word he used was that he beseeched me, and I've been sitting by the phone all morning waiting to be beseeched."

"(Laughter)"

QUESTION: "He said he sent you a copy of the press release this morning."

REAGAN: "Well, it evidently hasn't wended its way through the halls to reach me, but any time he wants to beseech me, I'm there."

QUESTION: "What will be your answer when he does?"

REAGAN: "What?"

QUESTION: "What will be your answer when he does?"

REAGAN: "It would have to be the same one I've given here, that I haven't had the chance to read it."

On the *state* open housing measure, the Rumford Act, Reagan was equally confusing. During his 1966 campaign, he stated without qualification that he would push for outright repeal of the Rumford Act. Once in office, he did nothing and would not even state his position on proposals to modify or revise the Rumford Act. That was one ugly, vote-winning campaign pledge that he weaseled out of, with vacillation and silence.

Reagan often seeks to justify his inaction on the needs of the minorities and the poor with the argument that there has been progress in the past decade or two. No one disputes that, but I have always regarded such argument as logically and morally shaky. In essence, the argument suggests that, because black Americans used to have about a third of the rights, opportunities, and income of white Americans and because they now have about half as many rights, opportunities, and income as whites—everybody ought to relax. Reagan adds an absurd and patronizing rationale for relaxation when he offers comparative statistics, as in this statement of July 8, 1969:

"As of now, the only country in the world where the white majority sends a greater percentage of young . . . Negroes to college and universities than in America is France. We actually send a higher percentage of Negroes to colleges and universities in America today than any other country in the world sends white people to those schools." (The second part of that statement is patently false.)

In his eagerness to avoid the responsibility of leadership to spur racial progress, the Governor has been either sloppy or cynical in his perversion of the truth. In 1967, he vetoed a federal antipoverty grant of $56,250 to provide beautification, parks, and open-space jobs in Ventura County for seventeen chronically jobless individuals. Reagan indignantly complained—once on a national television interview—that half of the grant would be eaten up for the salaries of seven administrators to oversee the modest project. The truth, however, as confirmed later by the Office of Economic Opportunity, was that only $3,640 of the federal grant was earmarked for overhead personnel—one half-time coordinator and a one-day-a-week payroll clerk.

California's problems of poverty and social tensions are not limited to black citizens, who comprise 7.5 per cent of the population and reside mainly in the larger cities. The state's Mexican-Americans, comprising 11.5 per cent of the total population, have suffered acutely from discrimination and poverty. In many of the measurements of economic and social disadvantage, California's Mexican-Americans are in worse shape than the state's blacks, partly because of the language barrier and particularly in the rural areas where many of them work as farm laborers. In the mid-1960's, the average Mexican-American farm-worker made $1,378 a year. Hunger, deplorable living conditions, poor health, and inadequate educational opportunities stifle the state's Mexican-Americans as much—or more—than blacks, a fact too often overlooked in the recent national concern and publicity for the plight of the Negro.

Reagan's approach to the problems of Mexican-Americans is every bit as negligent as his attitude toward blacks. His budget-slashing, war-on-welfare policies have slowed progress by both groups. If his governmental policies toward the needs of the Negro are reactionary, his official approach to the problems of Mexican-Americans in rural areas is feudalistic.

He has invariably sided with growers and corporate farmers against farm workers in struggles to improve conditions
for the workers. He shared the callous attitudes of Senator
George Murphy toward the "bracero" program—the importation of Mexican nationals at low wages to work in California fields. (Murphy, arguing against an end to the
"bracero" program, once said that Mexicans were more suitable for stoop labor in the fields than Americans because
"they are built differently.") Generally, Reagan has concerned himself more with the threat of violence by Mexican-
Americans than with the "root causes" of their discontent:
serflike working conditions and impoverished living conditions. On March 19, 1968, the Governor was asked about
rumors of rural violence:

QUESTION: "Governor, have you . . . had any indication at
all of any 'Brown Power' riots or disturbances scheduled for
the Central Valley on behalf of the Mexican-American population?"

REAGAN: "Well now, I haven't checked completely on this
recently. I do try to keep a finger on it, and we are observ-
ing all of these possibilities and threats. I was interested to
see that Mr. [Cesar] Chavez the other day made quite an
impassioned plea for nonviolence. . . ."

Reagan's attitude toward Cesar Chavez and his efforts to
organize farm workers reveals the hypocrisy and inconsistency of the Governor's public position on social progress.
Reagan damns violent tactics for change with angry rhetoric
about "lawbreakers and mad dogs." But when a minority
group seeks reform or progress through legal and peaceful
methods, he remains unmoved. The Governor not only refuses to commend the leaders of minority groups striving for
redress of "their legitimate grievances," but also impugns
their worth as leaders and opposes their specific and peaceful
actions.

Cesar Chavez is one of the great men of California today. He is as deeply committed to the progress of his people—Mexican-American and other farm workers—and to the principle of nonviolence as was Martin Luther King in the black struggle. He combines an almost saintly style of personal life with the tough leadership of a labor organizer. Chavez grew up in the farm fields of California, organized the National Farm Workers Association (NFWA) in the early 1960's, and led the partially successful strike of grape workers in the Delano area in the mid-1960's. In 1966, Reagan admitted that farm workers "have not obtained their fair share," but he stated flatly, "I am not in sympathy with the demonstrators in Delano." My own support for Chavez and the National Farm Workers Association was obscured in April, 1966, when Chavez led a march of workers to Sacramento and I did not comply with their request for a meeting in the Capitol on Easter Sunday. I had promised my family that I would spend Easter with them in Palm Springs and stuck by that family commitment. I realize now that that incident tarnished my reputation with the Chavez movement, despite my pledge to push for legislation giving the NFWA collective bargaining rights in California.

That was the central goal of Chavez, along with establishment of a minimum wage for farm workers, and he won support from organized labor and eventual recognition of the NFWA as a bargaining agent from some of the biggest growers and farm corporations in the state. But the progress, eked out by peaceful and nonviolent methods, was won, over the criticism and opposition of Ronald Reagan.

No man has been closer to the people he led than Chavez; few labor movements have ever had a "grass-roots" character as deep as Chavez's NFWA. But Reagan has denigrated both Chavez and the union and has refused to commend their nonviolent tactics. The Governor boasts about his former work as a labor official in the motion picture industry, but these were his comments in a press conference of March 19, 1968:

QUESTION: "Governor, do you support the principle of the Chavez movement, the unionized farm laborers, to give them bargaining power the same as other unions?"

REAGAN: "I have always said that certainly I can't be an opponent of organized labor, but I've always said that labor should be organized from the ranks of the workers themselves who want this. There is a great deal of evidence to indicate at this moment that he still does not speak for the overwhelming majority of those who are working in that field. [Many of them were scabs brought in by growers.] . . . I am opposed to the organizing of labor when it is done from the outside on the basis of a small clique." [Thousands of farm workers were formal members of the NFWA and all reliable reports confirmed that Chavez's movement had the overwhelming support of the workers.]

QUESTION: "Aren't your comments tantamount to saying that there shouldn't be unionization in the field. With a fluctuating labor force, how would it be possible for a union to be formed, except by a small group?"

REAGAN: ". . . Those who believe that you can impose on the farm economy the industrial type of union have failed to see some of the farmers' problems. [Chavez understood that; he successfully fought off an attempt by the Teamsters Union to organize farm workers.] While I have respected in the union the right to strike, I don't see how you could possibly have collective bargaining in the farm economy without some protection against calling a strike at harvest time, when there could be no legitimate bargaining and when there could be nothing but coercion and blackmail in such a strike."

Cutting through the evasive language, one can see that

Reagan was leaving no option at all to this deprived minority, which was seeking progress. If its members used violent tactics, they were "mad dogs and lawbreakers." If they used peaceful, legal methods, they were practicing "blackmail."

Reporters made a final attempt to get Reagan to clarify his attitude toward the nonviolent Chavez:

QUESTION: "As a labor man, how do you assess Chavez . . . as a farm labor leader?"

REAGAN: "Well, I've had some difficulty reconciling some of his statements with some of his next echelon and their actions. There has seemed to be a tendency toward disruption certainly on their part in spite of his words. And, again, I say it does not seem to be the grass roots type of organizing that I believe should take place."

On another issue largely related to Mexican-Americans, Reagan revealed that he is really far more concerned with sustaining the status quo of society than with the type of tactics used to affect change. Despite his occasional statements that minorities and others could use "legitimate channels" for change instead of violent tactics, he has steadily opposed a program to give the rural poor a greater chance for progress through the courts.

The California Rural Legal Assistance (CRLA) program was established, along with similar programs in other states, with federal funds to provide attorney services to the rural poor. In early 1968, a spokesman for the Reagan Administration said that the Governor opposed the entire concept of a federally financed staff of lawyers giving legal aid to the poor. He also said that "if the poor really need legal help," they should go to such private organizations as the American Civil Liberties Union or the National Association for the Advancement of Colored People. Reagan even threatened to veto the $1.5 million program, which, as Governor, he had the authority to do. He attacked CRLA with the claim that it was wasting money and handling legal cases improperly. But it was apparent that his real resentment against the program was that CRLA was filing cases on behalf of the rural poor *collectively* and was winning most of those cases in the courts. Two cases, both of which the CRLA won, particularly rankled Reagan. The first resulted in a court order preventing the importation of "bracero" farm workers. The second led to the State Supreme Court decision that Reagan's cutback of the state's Medi-Cal program was illegal.

The success of the CRLA attorneys on behalf of the rural poor also elicited this incredible response from Reagan's then top assistant, William P. Clark:

"The encouragement of litigation has perhaps opened the door too wide to the indigent client. They have imposed burdens on rural courts by their incursions into social legislation. This could be carried to all sorts of extremes."

In his press conference of October 3, 1967, Reagan magnanimously acknowledged the need for legal help to the poor involved in individual civil actions, but complained that CRLA had gone too far and "has kind of been a promoter of social causes." Reporters had trouble understanding or accepting Reagan's logic:

QUESTION: "Governor, in your attitude toward the Rural Legal Assistance Office, are you arguing that the poor should not use the courts to cause social change?"

REAGAN: "No, I think I answered that. Where there are individuals here who have a legitimate case and the inability for legal assistance, I think they should have this legal assistance."

QUESTION: "But not groups?"

REAGAN. "Well, let's take for example the Rural League of Assistance [he didn't even have the name right] getting into the case involving the importation of supplemental labor. I'm quite sure there are a great many citizens who feel completely the opposite of the position taken by the [CRLA] . . . but these citizens don't have the means to get the legal forces to buck the United States Government. . . ."

QUESTION: "Governor, in your speech in which you first criticized this outfit, you said they had been harassing the state and county governments in these court cases. Yet in some of these instances they are going to court and winning. Doesn't this sort of take away the harassment aspect if they are getting the judges agreeing with them?"

REAGAN: "There are a number of instances where they can also harass without winning, and . . . they have attracted this publicity and succeeded in delaying . . . something that needs to be done . . . [like] crop picking. . . ."

How does Reagan expect the poor, the Mexican-Americans, the blacks, and other minorities to progress toward more equal opportunities and better lives? How does he expect a lessening of the frustrations and tensions among minorities that are polarizing our society into two contending camps?

The Reagan record reveals only a series of negatives. He condemns violent tactics. But he also slashes budgets and scuttles programs of government to achieve progress for the minorities and the poor. He denounces court decisions that favor the minorities and the poor. He invariably opposes federal and even state legislation to end discrimination. He refuses to talk with or learn from any representatives of the minorities except those he patronizingly labels "responsible leaders." He condemns or mocks such peaceful, organized efforts as Cesar Chavez's Farm Workers Association and he denounces and threatens such proper, legal programs as the CRLA.

What's left for the minorities and the poor? Under Reagan, what hope do they have to break off the shackles of discrimination and poverty?

Reagan offers no answer to those questions, no substantial hope to the least fortunate citizens of society, no firm strategy that might restore peace and harmony to a fragmented state and nation. His only positive suggestion is little more than a naïve platitude: that somehow the people will voluntarily and individually help each other, through the "dynamics of the free enterprise system."

"You can pass a law," Reagan says, "but you don't change the heart of the individual who is discriminating. I think that people can be changed."

I, too, believe in America's free, capitalistic system. I agree that government by itself should not and cannot solve all the economic and social problems of the people. I would hope, along with Reagan, that the hearts of the people will change and would rejoice if the people voluntarily and spontaneously moved to end discrimination and poverty.

But a change of heart will not come about among the people unless the people are challenged by leaders committed to human progress, leaders who speak with persuasive compassion. In the informal, educational role of leadership, Reagan totally lacks such qualities. He has frequently reacted with indignation when his adversaries have expressed doubts about the depths of his humanitarian instincts. But the doubts are justified. Rarely and, then, vaguely, Reagan talks of "changing the hearts" of the people. But frequently and forcefully, he denounces those who truly work for humanitarian programs and goals as "bleeding-heart liberals."

Mistakes *have* been made by governments and "liberals" in their efforts to hasten progress for the minorities and poor of our society. Legislation has occasionally been careless and administration of new programs has often been sloppy. In their zeal to tackle long-neglected human problems in the nation, many political leaders have made excessive promises that unfairly heightened the expectations of deprived citizens. But the mistakes should be rectified and the promises modified, rather than junking the basic efforts and abandoning the goals of equality and justice for all Americans.

Unless today's leaders renew their commitment to the promises of the Constitution and their appeal to the deeper consciences of the American people, society's frustrated and deprived members will be left with only two, tragic choices—despair or violence. There must be a middle course between indifference and repression, a middle road between reactionary government and anarchic revolution. Reagan has not found the middle course, nor does he even seek the middle road of reform toward a just and peaceful society. And time is running out. The people—on all sides of today's social conflicts—are becoming increasingly dissatisfied and impatient, and all too ready to turn to extreme or arbitrary methods and measures to achieve change or stability. And clearly, the most acute and volatile impatience is today being felt and expressed by the young.

8

War on the Campus

The turmoil on the nation's campuses in recent years has either completely confused or totally antagonized a majority of Americans. The so-called generation gap, as it relates to the issue of campus unrest in California, is really more of a chasm, and it is approaching the dimensions of the Grand Canyon. A few penetrating insights offered by the National Commission on the Causes and Prevention of Violence provide the beginnings of a bridge of understanding. The Commission, chaired by Dr. Milton S. Eisenhower, made these observations in June, 1969:

"The problem of campus unrest is more than a campus problem. . . . There is no single cause, no single solution. We urge all Americans to reject hasty and simplistic answers. We urge them to distinguish between peaceful protest and violent disruption, between the nonconformity of youth and the terror tactics of the extremists. . . .

"Although much of the discontent often focuses on grievances within the campus environment, it is rooted in dis-
satisfactions with the larger society. . . .

"Students are unwilling to accept the gaps between pro-
fessed ideals and actual performance. They see afresh the
injustices that remain unremedied. . . . Today's intelligent,
idealistic students see a nation which has achieved the
physical ability to provide food, shelter, and education for
all, but has not yet devised social institutions that do so.
They see a society, built on the principle that all men are
created equal, that has not yet assured equal opportunity in
life. They see a world of nation-states with the technical
brilliance to harness the ultimate energy but without the
common sense to agree on methods of preventing mutual
destruction. . . .

"At a time when students are eager to attack these and
other key problems, they face the prospect of being compelled to fight in a war most of them believe is unjustified.
This traumatic experience has precipitated an unprecedented
mass tension and frustration. . . .

"Most students, despite their view of society's failures, accept as valid the basic structure of our democratic system;
their main desire is to improve its ability to live up to its
stated values. . . . A small but determined minority, however,
aims not at reform but at the destruction of existing institutions. These are the nihilists. They resort to violent disruption as the means best suited to achieve their ends. . . . When
they have managed on occasion to provoke counterforce to
an excessive degree, they have succeeded in enlisting the
sympathies of the more moderate campus majority. . . ."

There is another factor, an emotional factor, which has
contributed to the chasm between the generations and the
public disgust for student turmoil. In California, the students attending the state's universiy system are a minority

within society, an *advantaged* minority. Under the law of the state plan for higher education, only the top 12.5 per cent of high school graduates are academically eligible to attend any of the various campuses of the University of California. The minority group status applies also, to a lesser extent, to the students of the state colleges, which accept applications from the top third of the high school graduates. The majority of Californians end their education with a year or two in a junior college or even stop with graduation from high school. There is, as a result, a subtle element of jealousy within the majority of the California public toward the advantaged minority who attend the state colleges and universities. Time after time, I have heard this comment from indignant citizens: "*I* wasn't able to go to college; why don't those damn kids settle down and be grateful that they can go?"

My own educational experience gives me the basis for understanding this element of jealousy toward the advantaged minority of college and university students in California. I never attended a regular college or university. After high school, I was obligated to help my family financially. For a time, I worked in my father's photography store in San Francisco. Later I took a full-time job with the Pacific Gas and Electric Company. I would have preferred to attend the University of California or a state college, but instead continued my education with four years of night school. I was proud of the achievement of a law degree and admission to the bar as a practicing attorney, but I admit that through most of my life I've had a bit of an inferiority complex because I lacked a university education. (One of the most satisfying events of my life was when I, a night law-school graduate, addressed the Harvard Law School a few years ago. The sense of achievement at that moment helped me overcome the old inferiority complex.)

Because of this subtle personal hang up—this frustrated yearning for the academic world—there may have been times when, as Governor, I muffled my critical judgments of state university and college officials. But there was another and more powerful reason for my restraint in dealing with California's universities and colleges. As Governor, I was not only determined to provide the funds and leadership to establish the best system of higher education in the nation; I was also committed to keeping the universities and colleges free of the vagaries of political interference in their operations. The whole concept of the university—stemming from medieval times—is intrinsically involved with the concept of freedom. The National Commission headed by Dr. Eisenhower put it best: "Whenever the freedom of universities is in jeopardy, so is the freedom of the nation." Samuel Gould, President of the State University of New York, told his State Legislature: "A society that can no longer trust universities can no longer trust itself."

It is obvious that the majority of Californians today, egged on by the anti-intellectual rhetoric of Ronald Reagan, do not trust their universities and are contemptuous of the "minority" that are the university students. The war on the campus today is not just a battle between a few violently radical students and the police; it is an emotional conflict between Reagan and his supporters and the entire academic community. It is ironic that one of the first warnings of this pattern was uttered by Clark Kerr—*before* the first major outbreak of student disorder at Berkeley in 1964 and before Reagan and the Regents dumped him as University President. In *The Uses of the University*, Kerr wrote:

"Since, in the long run, progress is more important than peace to a university, the effective mediator must, at times, sacrifice peace to progress. . . . To make the multiversity work really effectively, the moderates need to be in control of each power center and there needs to be an attitude of tolerance between and among power centers. . . . When extremists get in control of the students, the faculty, or the trustees with class war concepts, then the 'delicate balance of interests' becomes an actual war."

The "actual war"—now nationwide—began on the campus of the University of California at Berkeley in the autumn of 1964. The issues and incidents of that first campus battle anywhere in the nation in recent history now seem, in retrospect, tame. It centered on a controversy between students and university administrators over the rights and rules of political activity on the campus. Specifically, it was precipitated when the Dean of Students told students that they could not set up pamphlet-covered tables, recruit members, raise funds, or make speeches for political or social action in the area outside of Sproul Hall, the university administration building. In protest, the Free Speech Movement (FSM) was born. It flourished on the campus, as the "tolerance" of which Kerr wrote broke down—along with negotiations between students and administrators—and was fed by the oratory of student Mario Savio. FSM leaders defied university regulations; several were suspended from school. Adopting the nonviolent techniques of civil rights protests in the South, hundreds of students staged a series of sit-ins in Sproul Hall. Thousands of students and many faculty members—went on strike against routine class operations. Tensions ran high and antagonism was acute, but there was virtually no violence. In the early morning of December 3— and on the request of University Chancellor Edward W. Strong—I ordered 600 officers of the Highway Patrol onto the campus to assist local police in ending the sit-in at Sproul Hall. About 800 students and others were arrested, then released on bail the next day. (Under emergency legislation, most of them were quickly tried in the courts and given misdemeanor penalties.) President Kerr and others continued to negotiate with FSM leaders, while publicly the issues of the controversy were partly obscured by excessive press attention to a few isolated instances of "filthy speech" defiance. A month after the breakup of the sit-in, the Board of Regents replaced Chancellor Strong with Martin Meyerson (now President of the University of Pennsylvania). The next day, January 3, the new Chancellor announced provisional rules that permitted open political discussion—and tables—in the area in front of Sproul Hall. The Berkeley campus returned, for the moment, to "normal" academic operations.

But the war has continued, in episodic fashion, at Berkeley, spread to other campuses in the state and throughout the nation, and escalated into violence in recent years. The issues have varied, but few major campuses in the nation have been left untouched. Even that citadel of reason, Harvard University, was disrupted by violent clashes between students and authorities. And such reputedly conservative, "country club"-type campuses as the University of California at Santa Barbara have erupted into violence and arson that extended to adjoining communities. (In the Santa Barbara riots, in early 1970, extremist, nihilistic students burned down a Bank of America branch and several other business offices.)

The majority of the public, in California and nationally, have become incensed by the increasingly violent pattern of campus disorders. The campus crisis cries out for moderate, forceful, calm political leadership. Instead, it has all too often been accelerated by politicians who merely join the angry majority chorus in denouncing the "damn kids"—as if all students were part of some monolithic conspiracy—and in urging tough, hard-headed repression. That political stance undoubtedly wins votes. It does not ease the tensions or restore any reason to the campus conflicts.

The Berkeley issue was one of the main factors in my defeat by Reagan in the gubernatorial election of 1966. As a candidate, I was caught in the same political vise that has squeezed many moderate or liberal incumbents out of office. The growing number of indignant conservatives in the state were against me because I had not appeared to be tough enough in cracking down on student disorder during the Free Speech Movement. The ultraliberals and more militant allies of the students were against me because I had called out extra police to end the sit-ins. It was one example of the dilemma faced today by the moderate political leader who seeks to conciliate among warring factions.

Reagan, as a gubernatorial candidate in 1966, was not caught in the dilemma. He gave the angry majority what it wanted—an angry voice speaking for authority and order and against the troublesome students. Reagan simply picked sides in the conflict and, despite an occasional vague disclaimer, made it clear to the public that he would crack down on student dissidents. He added his own special touches in the campaign of 1966: I was "soft" on student disorder, university faculty members were often lazy, research-preoccupied agitators, and university administrators were vacillating appeasers. Above all, he left voters with the unqualified impression that he would stop what he repeatedly called "mob violence."

For awhile after his inauguration, Reagan still insisted—in general terms—that he would stop campus disorders. In a November, 1967, speech in Anaheim, the Governor pledged that his administration stood "ready to move at a moment's notice to stop riots before they start." The principal function of government, he declared, "is to protect society from the lawbreaker."

But the war on the state's campuses expanded. Berkeley barely got its breath back after the end of one crisis when another erupted. San Francisco State College was torn by an almost uninterrupted series of disorders. As one campus temporarily cooled, another burst into turmoil. The war moved to San José State College, to the University of California at Los Angeles, to San Diego State College. In the past four years, virtually every major campus in the state has been the scene of increasingly violent disorder. The sequence of disturbances reached tragic proportions with the People's Park battle at Berkeley in the spring of 1969 (1 dead, more than 200 injured) and the riots at Santa Barbara in early 1970 (millions of dollars of damage to local businesses).

Logically and politically, Reagan by all odds should have been in a tough and difficult spot. He had won election, in part, by exploiting public impatience over a *single* major campus disturbance during my administration, the FSM trouble at Berkeley in 1964. He had pledged to crack down on student disorders and stop the campus turmoil. But, during his administration, the war broke out scores of times on dozens of campuses. Reagan did not *cause* the campus disorders from 1967 through 1970, no more than I deserved the blame for the trouble at Berkeley in 1964. But he managed to avoid public displeasure and to gloss over the flat pledges he had made during the 1966 campaign and early in his first year as Governor. His political strategy was simple. He abandoned the shaky reasoning of 1966 that placed responsibility for campus peace in the lap of the Governor. As Governor, his reasoning found a new scapegoat for the war on the campuses: university administrators.

In December, 1967, while San Francisco State College was in turmoil, Reagan said: "In this state more than any other state that I know of, there are great restrictions as to what the governmental authorities can do." Again and again, he repeated the theme that the Governor and state government had no authority or responsibility relating to campus disorders. By February, 1969, during another episode of disruption and violence at Berkeley, Reagan had polished his scapegoating tactic to a fine art and completely abandoned his attitude of 1966. At his press conference of February 25, he said:

"The issue has to be solved by the university administration itself. And it will not be solved until they are ready to use their own powers to separate from the campus if need be either faculty or students who insist upon this kind of disorder. Until they are willing to do this, all we can look forward to is having a kind of armed camp protecting the rights of the majority who want to get an education. This is right in the lap of the college and university administrators now. . . . The resolution of the conflict is in the administrators' hands."

Faced by a rising wave of campus turmoil during his administration, Reagan had seen the light—and apparently he had finally read the State Constitution. Except for the appointment of Regents and his own membership on that Board, the Governor of California is prohibited from any direct involvement in the operation of state universities and colleges. His only *formal* authority related to a campus disorder is to call out state police or the National Guard—but only when the help is requested by local officials. Reagan did this often and eagerly as Governor, as the campus war escalated beyond the capacities of college and local law enforcement personnel.

But a Governor does have—beyond his limited legal authority—immense influence of an informal sort. The effect of his voice and words—as the highest elected official of the state—is powerful, particularly on an issue as controversial and emotional as campus turmoil. In the passions of student discontent, radical agitation, and public impatience, the temper and tone of the Governor's statements can be critically influential.

My policy as Governor on any volatile campus disorder

was to comply with local requests for law enforcement help, to back up the decisions of authorities at the scene, to counsel restraint, to speak briefly and calmly about the crisis— and then keep my mouth shut. In any actual or threatened campus disruption, I was keenly aware of the delicate and dangerous tensions running and the overabundance of defiant, angry denunciations on both sides of the conflict. I was determined not to add any heat, through my words or deeds, to the developing campus war. My opposition to lawlessness or violent tactics was well known, so I kept my rhetoric restrained.

In effect, Reagan declared and sustained verbal warfare toward the entire academic community of California—the student "mob," the "agitating" professors, the "vacillating" administrators, and the "appeasing" chancellors. His denunciations were invariably generalized. When challenged by reporters to identify actual examples of "appeasement" or individual "vacillating" administrators, he would weasel away from "specifics." Occasionally, he would speak magnanimously about the majority of "responsible and orderly" students and professors, but so parenthetically and so briefly that the comments seldom gained much public attention. Reagan is perceptive enough about the workings of the news media to know that his blanket, angry condemnations—not his mild, occasional disclaimers—would get the headlines and public attention. The total effect of his public rhetoric and propaganda on campus disorders—as on so many other issues —has been to plant the simplistic good guys—bad guys theme on the public consciousness, thus adding fuel to the fiery passions on the campuses.

He has seldom, if ever, been conciliatory in the conflicts. On June 3, 1969, while the People's Park crisis in Berkeley was still tense, he rigidly opposed the suggestions of some civic officials and university officers (and the editor of *The*

San Francisco Chronicle) for a compromise between the university and the young:

QUESTION: "Governor Reagan, are you personally receptive to the idea that the Regents lease a portion of People's Park to the City of Berkeley, which in turn presumably would sublease it to the street people?"

REAGAN: ". . . I am totally, as a Regent and as a Governor, opposed to anything that would in any way be a subterfuge to go around and give to these people any kind of face-saver." In that statement, Reagan also invoked one of his favorite, derisive labels for the bad guys; he was against surrendering to the "blackmailers."

A few weeks later, still being questioned on the People's Park conflict, Reagan again revealed his negative attitude toward conciliation and mediation of a crisis. He was sharply critical of Berkeley Chancellor Roger Heyns, who had worked desperately to calm the conflict. "He made . . . more efforts than I would have made to conciliate and negotiate with these people," the Governor said. Reagan was asked to comment on a story that Chancellor Heyns was about to resign. Reporters were so clearly aware of his contempt for Heyns that they burst into laughter when he said that he had "heard no talk of resignation" and would be sorry to see Heyns leave. His hypocrisy on that question couldn't cover up his apparent reversal of a noble Biblical injunction. "Damned be the Peacemakers, for they shall be fired" is not a substantial exaggeration of the Reagan attitude.

His rigid stance, his simplistic instinct to join one side of a conflict was unwavering during the People's Park battle in Berkeley. There was no question that the controversy stemming from the use of a university-owned vacant lot by Berkeley "street people" and students as a park escalated into violence as the result of mistakes, confusion, and intransigence on all sides. Some nihilistic agitators abused the

People's Park issue as a ploy for confrontation with authorities. Some of the young people taunted police, and a few broke windows in the area and threw bricks at sheriff's deputies. University officials and civic authorities misjudged the tense situation and failed to find a solution. But it was also starkly evident that law enforcement personnel often acted with excessive and unjustified brutality. Mayor Joseph Alioto of San Francisco, who had helped resolve one crisis at San Francisco State College with the measured and restrained use of police, labeled the performance of law enforcement personnel on the People's Park battle as "amateur night in Berkeley." The indiscriminate use of shotguns (with both bird-shot and buckshot) resulted in death for one man, blindness for another, and dozens of serious injuries. For the first time in American history, a state conducted an aerial attack on civilians when a sheriff's officer sent a National Guard helicopter over the campus to spew tear gas. The gas not only sickened and terrified student demonstrators, but also university employees and patients in a nearby hospital. The sloppy roundup and arrests of several hundred young people—and their subsequent mistreatment at a nearby detention center—resulted in only a few convictions and, a year later, federal indictments against several sheriff's deputies.

How did Reagan react? He continued, in broad generalities, to condemn "the mob" of students and defended the law enforcement personnel. The blatantly brutal tactics of some of the sheriff's officers, the death of a young man, the gas-spewing helicopter? He shrugged them off without comment or a "that's-the-way-the-ball-bounces-in-war" remark.

The critical judgment of police tactics during the People's Park battle is not just my own. On May 30, *The Los Angeles Times* said in an editorial:

"They played into the hands of the revolutionaries by a

use of repressive force beyond any order of magnitude required. As a result, those whom the law was supposed to protect were given cause to distrust and fear the law. . . . Authorities will have to be far more discriminating in their response than they have been, to avoid harming those who have done no wrong. Failure in this area makes constituted authority the unwitting ally of violence-prone militants. When that hapepns, where does it leave the rest of society?"

The *Sacramento Bee* was particularly angered by the mass arrests during the battle. It commented on July 11:

"So methodical was the herding of a crowd into a closed area that it appeared to be planned repression rather than on-the-spot enforcement of the law. The aftermath of this military exercise now discloses how inept and unnecessary was the tactic. All 416 of the mass arrest cases have been dismissed in court."

Such developments, I am convinced, are the result, in part, of Reagan's jingoistic, shoot-from-the-hip "law and order" rhetoric.

Reagan's reaction to the various demonstrations against Vietnam war policies in recent years is reminiscent of the hysteria of the Joseph McCarthy era in the early 1950's. Those demonstrations, sometimes bursting into violence but most often peaceful, elicited contempt from Reagan. In October, 1967, he said that Communists were spurring the antiwar demonstrations that were beginning to sweep across the United States and several other nations. Reagan said in Des Moines, Iowa, "We'd be pretty naïve to rule out the part Communists play in these demonstrations." In the same month and in other speeches, the Governor clearly alleged "treason" in antiwar demonstrations and then—in irresponsible indifference to several delicate questions of international law and diplomacy—said:

"There would be plenty of laws to cover them [the demonstrators] if we were technically in a state of war." Pressed by reporters, Reagan stopped short of urging a declaration of war against North Vietnam but suggested that it might be possible to "implement the same rules" against antiwar protestors. Backed into a logical corner, he did finally acknowledge that such "treason" laws and rules should not be applied to peaceful demonstrators.

On such issues, Reagan not only ventured ignorantly into the legal realm, but also demagogically delved into the emotions of the public. On October 26, 1967, he said:

"I don't think the American people can continue to buy their sons' being asked to fight and die while that same government defends the right of the dissenter to take his dissent into actually aiding the enemy that's trying to kill their sons."

Contrary to the admonition of the Eisenhower Commission on violence, Reagan seldom made any attempt to "distinguish between peaceful protest and violent disruption, between the nonconformity of youth and the terror tactics of extremists." He angrily condemned antiwar demonstrators at the Oakland Induction Center in the fall of 1967, but made no distinction between those few who precipitated violence and the thousands who earlier assembled there peacefully, legally, and nonviolently. During the People's Park conflict in Berkeley in 1969, he denounced those students who used violent tactics—which was understandable—but continually condemned "the mob" of student demonstrators—which was inflammatory. He refused to give any credit at all to the tens of thousands of students, other young people, and Berkeley area residents who expressed their sympathy for People's Park in peaceful demonstration. On Friday, May 30, an estimated 50,000 people marched in silent, peaceful protest against the excesses of police tactics or in support of the People's Park project. Their leaders worked with city officials and received authorization for the march and also organized teams of monitors to discourage any violence-advocating troublemakers among the throng. In a tense and volatile atmosphere, those tens of thousands of people marched several miles through Berkeley's narrow streets without a single incident of trouble. Reagan was asked about that peaceful demonstration at his press conference of June 3:

QUESTION: "Does the size and makeup of the demonstration in Berkeley last Friday give you any second thoughts about the size and makeup of the so-called dissident minority, which you say is challenging the university?"

REAGAN: "No, not at all. These people have been very successful in their efforts always to cloud an issue and to try to get some innocent people involved who would not understand what was really at stake. . . . There is no question but that there are a large number of people who misunderstood. . . . I don't blame the kids for getting confused, for joining in a parade of the kind that was held last Friday."

Reagan condemned and denounced "the mob" of students for lawless or violent tactics. But, when vast numbers of students and others used legal and peaceful means of expressing themselves, they were, at best, "confused," in the Governor's judgment. He acknowledged no "legitimate grievance" by students on a specific issue that led to conflict. He left no logical alternative to the student who wanted to be heard but did not want to engage in violent tactics.

After each campus disturbance in California in recent years, Reagan has proclaimed, in an increasingly angry voice, his basic policy and attitude toward disorder: "Obey the rules or get out!" He insistently urged college and university administrators to suspend or dismiss any student who broke campus regulations.

Yet he was almost equally impatient with student demonstrations that conformed to law and campus rules. On

May 17, 1968, about 2,000 students gathered in front of Sproul Hall in Berkeley for an antidraft protest. Protest leaders earlier had been denied permission to use the campus's Greek Theater, but were authorized by the university to stage the rally in Sproul Plaza. Reagan heard about the plans and fired off a letter to University President Charles Hitch asking that the rally be prohibited, that the charter of the sponsoring group be revoked, and that faculty members involved be disciplined. Hitch refused, and the rally was conducted peacefully. Chancellor Heyns reported to the Regents and the press on the rally: "All university regulations were obeyed. . . . There was no abrasiveness, no misconduct, no soliciting of pledges to refuse to register for the draft. . . . The meeting was completely within the law and all university regulations were obeyed." Reagan ignored the report and the facts. The rally, he said, "was beneath contempt" and had been allowed only on a "technicality." The Governor's conduct in that instance—and many others —mocked his rare statements in support of "peaceful dissent."

After another, but disruptive, demonstration at San Jose State College, Reagan was almost livid about the "appeasement" of campus administrators toward black students protesting discrimination there. Dr. Robert Clark, San Jose State President, judged that the situation on his campus in September, 1967, was so tense over the threat of racial violence that he canceled the first football game of the season. The right-wing Max Rafferty, State Superintendent of Public Instruction, raged: "If I had to ask the President to call in the whole United States Marine Corps, that game would have been played." Reagan, only slightly less demagogic and graphic in his comments, said that he was against "yielding" and was for "calling out the necessary force and law enforcement" to let the football game be played. On that occasion, Rafferty pre-empted Reagan's use of his choice phrase. "I wouldn't have submitted," Rafferty said. "I don't like blackmail."

As the campus disorders spread, Reagan at times seemed ambivalent about his authority as Governor to deal with them. After one meeting to discuss troubles on the state college campuses, Reagan complained that he and the administrators could charge students with inciting to violence, but "technically and legally you can't make it stick." In the next breath, he said to newsmen "I can assure you that when violence starts it will be met by force."

After another meeting with University of California Regents, Reagan spoke in anger and frustration. Referring to incidents of demonstrations and disruption at Los Angeles, Berkeley, Santa Barbara, and San Diego, the Governor cried anew that the university (with authority over all of those campuses) was on the "sorry road of appeasement that leads to more and more of the same thing."

He also proposed steps that clearly could be labeled repressive. After one small group of students displayed a North Vietnamese emblem during an antiwar protest, the Governor urged the Regents to ask for new legislation to prohibit antiwar demonstrations. At another point, he urged that any faculty members involved in incidents that *resulted* in any violence should be barred from teaching at any campus in the state. He joined the rush of other politicians in suggesting a variety of repressive laws, many of them of extremely doubtful Constitutionality. One Reagan proposal asked for a law permitting the immediate arrest of any formerly suspended or expelled student who returned to the campus. He also suggested that students be issued "identity cards" that would permit them to enter a campus and use its facilities.

One of the few Reagan statements during the period with which I agreed was his comment: "I think there is a certain sense of unreality about the whole thing."

As with so many other controversial and complex issues, the Governor refused to inform himself in depth on the problem. In his press conference of June 24, 1969, he was pointedly asked why he had not appointed a "panel of distinguished citizens" to prepare a report on campus disorders:

REAGAN: "No, I don't think there would be any reason for this. The official reports are available."

QUESTION: "Well, not to be critical, but since your staff members work for you, might not the public assume that they would accept your point of view on this?"

REAGAN: ". . . From the first moment on, I had staff members over there [Berkeley] to bring me factual accounts of what was going on. I don't have a view in advance. . . . If local law enforcement in some incident is wrong, I'm not out to defend and endorse them. . . ."

Several days earlier, however, Reagan had defended and endorsed police tactics—including the helicopter attack and the use of shotguns—in his report on the People's Park battle to the Commonwealth Club of California.

As campus disorder has spread and escalated into more violence in California, Reagan's political popularity has not declined. In this era of fast-moving events and change, the people seem to forget quickly the words and actions of their political leaders. The majority of Californians obviously have forgotten the pledges of Reagan in 1966 and 1967 to stop campus disorder. Preoccupied with graphic, contemporary events, they have overlooked the past contradictions in Reagan's record on the campus war. He echoes and amplifies their impatience, anger, and contempt for campus disorder and doesn't burden them with challenges to understand all the many complex or obscure causes of student discontent. His service to the people on this issue is not leadership. His disservice is a jingoistic simplification of a conflict that is dividing society. And the most tragic consequence of Reagan's role on the campus war is the public designation of scapegoats for the crisis. Reagan's successful scapegoating on this issue goes beyond the justified denouncements of violence-advocating nihilists on the campuses. The sum effect of his harsh and hasty pronouncements is a rising tide of public disdain not just for bearded student radicals, but for student dissent itself. Reagan rarely praises the great work of the university. The public today is impatient not just with "vacillating" university administrators, but with the university and college system itself.

The Reagan-led majority in California has embarked on a dangerous and paradoxical path, partly as a result of its revulsion over the campus war. In a state with more diversity than any other in the nation, diverse attitudes and open dissent are now suspect. In a state that had built the finest system of higher education in the world, the university itself is now the scapegoat target for public reaction, repression, and reprisal.

9

War on Education

Education is by far the most important service of state government in California. Through most of the state's history, about half of each annual budget has been devoted to support for schools, colleges, and universities. The pattern is no accident. California's constitution declares explicitly that education must be given the highest financial priority, that educational services must have first claim on available state funds.

In his lengthy inaugural address in January, 1967, Governor Reagan devoted just three brief paragraphs to the subject of education—and those few comments merely repeated his threats to students to "obey the rules or get out" and challenged teachers to "build character on accepted moral and ethical standards."

But, in other statements and actions, Reagan more than

compensated for the lack of attention to education in his inaugural speech. Within a few weeks of becoming Governor, he virtually declared war on the state's educational system. The first attack, of course, was launched against the University of California, which—despite the recent incidence of student turmoil—remained one of the greatest institutions of learning in the world.

Reagan's attack on the university was not unexpected. Eight months before he became Governor, he threatened in a speech in San Jose:

"I am sick at what has happened at Berkeley. Sick at the sit-ins, the teach-ins, the walkouts. When I am elected Governor, I will organize a throw-out, and Clark Kerr will head that list."

For a very few days after the inauguration, Reagan pretended a degree of dignity on the issue. At his first press conference in early January, he stated that he had no "fixed idea" of the future of University President Kerr. Less than two weeks later, Kerr was fired. Reagan, slightly embarrassed by press criticism of political interference with the university, argued that his was only one out of fourteen votes by the Regents to fire Kerr. It is true that some conservative members of the Board of Regents had also tabbed Kerr as the ultimate example of a "vacillating administrator" and were ready to vote against him. But they would not have had the necessary margin without the influence and votes of Reagan, his new Lieutenant Governor, Robert Finch, and one other new member appointed by him.

Reagan attacked the California university system quickly in other ways, but not without a bit of public vacillation of his own. In the first few weeks of his term, his administration initially denied Sacramento rumors that he favored a 10 per cent cut in the budgets of the university and the state colleges. Before the end of the month, Reagan's economy ax slashed even more deeply than the rumors had suggested it would. In his first budget message to the legislature, the new Governor proposed these drastic reductions:

• A cut in the state appropriation for the University of California from the $278 million requested by the Board of Regents to $196.8 million—a *twenty-nine* per cent reduction.

• A cut in the appropriation for state colleges from the $213 million asked by the Board of Trustees to $154 million —a *twenty-eight* per cent reduction.

The news media correctly reported that Reagan's program would mean a radical shift in state policy: Qualified high school graduates would no longer be assured a place in California's institutions of higher learning. And some newspapers, including the *Sacramento Bee,* correctly noted a tragic irony in the Governor's policy for higher education: Reagan, who had campaigned under an "Obey the Law" banner, was defying both the state law spelling out the master plan for education and the Constitution itself. He was undeterred, arguing that he was just "cutting the fat" from the university and college operations, and that the money for the requested budgets "just isn't there."

Those who looked closely at the Governor's performance —and remembered his recent statements about education— saw through his arguments. There was enough money "there" for Reagan to take such non-economy steps as doubling the costs of his personal staff and office operations and of giving additional tax breaks to oil corporations operating in California. And critics knew that reductions of 28 and 29 per cent were more like chopping the heart out of higher education than "cutting the fat." The fears increased as Reagan uttered a series of statements that exposed an intrinsically anti-education attitude. Speaking directly within the context of a discussion on the higher education budget, Reagan said that he was not going to ask the taxpayers to help "subsidize intellectual curiosity." That incredible comment prompted this angry, but apt, response from a professor at UCLA: "What the hell does he think a university is all about?"

Kerr's firing and the budget cuts (which were only partially modified after negotiations with the Regents) were not the only prongs of Reagan's attack on higher education. He proposed another drastic measure to end the established and worthy principle of free higher education in California, urging that university and college students pay tuition for the first time in a century. The tuition proposal was advanced of course, with arguments about "economy."

In more outspoken moments, Reagan revealed another motivation for the tuition proposal. While Max Rafferty was beating the demagogic drums around the state by saying that Berkeley offered "a four-year course in sex, drugs, and treason," Reagan was saying that tuition would help keep "undesirables" out of Berkeley and other university campuses. "Those there to agitate and not to study might think twice before they pay tuition," he said at one press conference.

Within one month of becoming Governor, Reagan had thus come up with a neat trilogy of reprisal-type moves, which would affect those he and the public had stereotyped as scapegoats for campus turmoil: First, Kerr's firing could not but help intimidate other "vacillating" administrators. Second, the budget slashes and other fiscal decisions would penalize all those "agitating" professors. Third, tuition charges would hit all those noisy, sign-carrying student demonstrators. The formal proposals were advanced in the name of economy and necessity, of course. But on television and in his stump speeches, Reagan cleverly and subtly boasted that he was indeed cracking down on the troublesome campuses of the state.

By the end of that first month of what the *Sacramento*

Bee labeled Reagan's "ruthless" measures, I was shocked by his attack on higher education in the state. He had done about everything destructive possible except, perhaps, to invite commercial lumber interests to log the beautiful groves of trees off of the university campuses.

The shocked reaction was not confined to Reagan's political opponents or members of the academic communities. *The Los Angeles Times* became an articulate voice against his attack on higher education. In a January, 1967, editorial, *The Times* put the issue into proper perspective, referring to California's "great system of higher education and the unrivaled opportunity it offers to every qualified student." *The Times* noted that California had "achieved its tremendous technological growth and resulting prosperity primarily because of its unrivaled resources of higher education and university-connected research" and warned that endangering those resources "would be the most short-sighted and destructive kind of economizing."

By March 5, *The Times* had lost all respect for Reagan on the issue of higher education. A lengthy and carefully documented editorial stated:

"He has demonstrated that he does not believe it is vital for society to enable each citizen to achieve the best in knowledge and skill of which he is capable. . . . An anti-intellectual political reactionary now governs California and is determined to bring higher education growth to a grinding halt. . . . If a university is not a place where intellectual curiosity is to be encouraged and subsidized, then it is nothing. . . . If the Governor is seeking to transform the University of California overnight into an institution of second rank, and if he desires to hold back the development of a strong state college system, he has chosen the right paths to reach those goals."

But Reagan was basically unmoved by the criticism (though occasionally infuriated by it), and he adamantly pursued the path of devastating budget slashes and imposition of tuition. Starting in 1967, tens of millions of dollars were cut from the budget requests for the university and college systems. The State Legislature invariably approved larger and more appropriate sums; Reagan won out by use of the powerful "item veto" after legislative action. The Board of Regents at first voted against Reagan's tuition proposal, but gradually Reagan's war beat down the Regent's opposition on that issue. In the fall of 1967, the Board approved a slight increase in student "fees." The subject at times was confused publicly by an asinine argument over semantics—whether to call increased charges to students "fees" or "tuition." Three years after he opened the battle for tuition, the Governor was victorious. New tuition charges of up to $680 a year more than doubled the previous "fees" for all students at the university.

Throughout his term, Reagan kept insisting that tuition would not impose any hardship on students and that his deep budget cuts would not really effect the quality of higher education. His euphoric logic was absurd. Somehow it could not penetrate Reagan's closed mind that hundreds of dollars in extra tuition charges meant the difference between going to college or not for thousands of students. (Two-thirds of all university students were already working in full- or part-time jobs to pay their way.) And he was simply far removed from reality by thinking that orders for budget cuts of 20 per cent or more would not diminish the quality of learning in the universities and colleges.

University Regent Frederick Dutton clarified some of the real effects of tuition. It would, he estimated, "trigger a major property tax increase by forcing up to 14,000 students to turn to community colleges dependent on property taxes, instead of going to state colleges or the university, which rely on the state general fund."

There were other, more obvious and tragic results. Thousands of qualified, eligible students have been turned away from California's colleges in the past few years. In August, 1969, the *Sacramento Bee* reported and commented:

"In the field of higher education the Reagan program is disgraceful. California's once lauded excellence in providing opportunities for all qualified students to go to college has been diminished.

"The sad situation at the Sacramento State College is a case in point. SSC officials have turned away 1,125 applicants for admission this fall, . . . 85 to 95 per cent of them qualified. The rejection of these students marked the first time in the twenty-year history of the college qualified applicants were denied. . . .

"Compounding the picture is the fact there is no other institution of higher learning nearby that can handle the turn-aways. Only one of the eighteen state colleges is still accepting applications—in Fresno. . . .

"The Reagan Administration with its lack of concern for the plight of the thousands of students who cannot get into college may go down in history as the one that ruined this state's system of higher education so badly it will take years to recuperate."

In other areas of the state, the situation was worse. *The San Francisco Examiner* reported on September 29, 1969, that between 8,000 to 10,000 *eligible* students were turned away from San Francisco State College for that term.

The Reagan Administration argued that students turned away from one college could attend another that was less crowded—ignoring the fact that thousands of students would not be able to afford college if they had to move to another area and could not live at home. And the Board of Governors of the California Community Colleges (two-year junior colleges) declared, in September, 1969, that their entire system would break down unless community college graduates could be assured of admission to state colleges.

Several estimates indicated that more than 40,000 qualified, eligible applicants would be turned away from state
colleges by the fall of 1970.

The University of California, with nine campuses in various areas of the state, desperately and barely handled most
qualified applicants. But on February 6, 1970, after Reagan
cut the Regents budget from $374 million to $344 million,
The San Francisco Chronicle reported:

"University of California President Charles J. Hitch yesterday bit the bullet and said the university can live with the
budget proposed by Governor Ronald Reagan. . . .

"But Hitch said the Reagan budget provides no funds 'for
improving existing programs, and no funds for new programs, which means that we are prevented from carrying out
effectively one of our primary roles—the pursuit of new
knowledge.'

"Hitch noted the budget does not contain enough construction funds to meet growth demands. . . . 'Last year we
received less than 35 per cent of our very carefully considered capital request. This year that meager percentage
has dropped to less than 20 per cent.' . . .

"Hitch warned that if the situation continues over a
period of years, it will be 'impossible to provide facilities
for all qualified students in the decade of the 1970's.' "

The drastic reductions of university and college budgets
not only indicated Reagan's irritation with past events on the
campuses; he was being blind to the future—the near future.
Though California's total population growth has slowed
slightly in recent years, it is still adding hundreds of thousands of new residents every year. And the part of the population that is growing at the fastest rate is the school-age
group. Reagan may think that he is merely retaliating against
current student "troublemakers" or trimming fiscal "fat."
But the innocent are suffering now as a result of diminished
quality of education in the university and college systems,

and, during the next several years—at least—growing numbers of able young men and women just won't be able to get into the universities and colleges.

To me, Reagan's indifference to the future growth of California is the height of political and governmental irresponsibility. In California, a Governor *must* look ahead and prepare for the predictable needs of the people. One satisfaction I felt as I left the Governor's office was that my administrations had seen and prepared for the growing needs for higher education. From 1959 through 1966, we built three new campuses of the University of California and added eight new state colleges. Both the quality of education and the physical capacities of the campuses were keeping pace with the needs of our young people. It took money, planning, and long-range commitments to do the job.

My commitment to protecting and building California's system of higher education was both personal and pragmatic, sentimental and toughly realistic. On the issue of tuition, for example, I *know* that those extra hundreds of dollars are critical to the young men and women not supported by wealthy parents. My wife Bernice, her brother, and three sisters all went to the University of California at Berkeley. They were the children of a San Francisco police captain, who earned a modest salary. Each of them lived at home and commuted—by ferry boat, streetcar, and train—every day to Berkeley for three or four years. They could not have achieved that advanced education if tuition had been charged.

My support for tuition-free higher education was strengthened on less personal grounds. The money the state spends on higher education is the best investment possible—and not just toward humanitarian goals. Every reliable survey confirms that a college education substantially boosts the income of a citizen during his lifetime. A Californian with an academic degree will earn far more money each year than one who has stopped his education after high school. And he will (with his own increasing complaints) pay more in taxes. The state, with the graduated income tax, gets back in tax revenue what it spent earlier for college and university services. To dramatize this pragamatic point, I offer a hypothetical idea of the solid investment value of education: If I had some extra money for a long-range investment and could subsidize the costs of college for ten bright young men, I'd do it—if they agreed to return to me a percentage of their higher incomes after college. Indirectly, that's what happens when the state appropriates money for the college and university systems. It's a better *financial* investment, I am convinced, than buying real estate.

The economic advantages of a sound system of higher education are diverse. In an editorial criticizing Reagan's education budget cuts, *The San Francisco Chronicle* noted:

"If the university and state colleges are the primary source of leadership that brings . . . research and development funds to California, that is certainly one of the strongest reasons for the state's recognizing that its higher education system should be kept strong." *The Chronicle* added that education and research generates more jobs (and California needs them; its unemployment rate is generally higher than the rest of the nation) and that about a third of the billions spent for federal research and development programs come to California. Research funds go to those places that have the talent, and California's scientific and educational talent is unsurpassed. Almost *half* of America's Nobel Prize winners are in California. Dr. W. K. H. Panofsky, the director of the Stanford Linear Accelerator Center (Stanford is a private university), said in 1967: "There is no doubt in my mind that the primary reason for California's leadership in scientific and technical talent lies in its state university and state colleges."

California's magnificent research resources do much more than just draw federal funds into the state. That research is constantly paying off in ways that directly improve the state's economy. California's agriculture, for example, is the most modern, efficient, and productive in the world—in large measure because of the agricultural techniques developed through research at the University of California at Davis and other campuses. Radically new and more efficient harvesting machines and farming methods created at Davis have stimulated the economy of the state—and helped produce more food for a hungry nation and world.

Reagan basically ignores such immense benefits of the state's higher education system. One of his favorite negative platform themes is to downgrade the importance of research. The exaggerated image he draws for a suspicious public is of an absent-minded professor who doesn't like to teach and instead sits in ivy-towered seclusion indulging his "intellectual curiosity." There are legitimate and controversial questions about the research versus teaching roles of university and college staffs, but instead of just doubting the research role and damning higher education, Reagan ought to recognize publicly that both research and teaching are essential functions of a university. And instead of attacking a whole university and college system for the contemptuous actions of troublemakers, he ought to be praising the contributions of the university to California's economy, prosperity, and people.

The Governor's "economy" approach to higher education in California is of the most false and narrow variety. With his ruthless cuts of university and college budgets Reagan is worse than the kind of politician who can't look beyond the current fiscal year. Reagan barely looks beyond tomorrow morning's headlines—which he wins regularly with his spectacular "economy" crackdowns.

Reagan's war against the academic community—the budget slashes, the harassment of administrators, the constant public statements downgrading research and threatening other crackdowns—has halted progress in getting the best people to staff the universities and colleges. As early as the spring of 1967, the *Sacramento Bee* reported the university's increasing difficulties in the recruitment—and retention—of faculties. On April 12, *The Bee* reported:

"The University . . . and the state college system are having more difficulty seeking faculty members than they have ever had before.

"At the University of California at Davis there were several men who appeared to be sure additions to the campus faculty for the 1967–68 academic year. At the last moment, they backed out and refused to sign contracts."

The Bee report cited specific examples. A University of Tennessee faculty member being recruited for the Davis Medical School wrote this comment when he turned down the job: "The present turmoil in the University of California tends to cool many of us toward potential appointments until the situation has been clarified." One prominent historian turned down a UC appointment; the recruiter said later: "In a phone call, Professor _____ declined . . . to join our faculty because of the firing of Kerr and probable further difficulties facing the university in securing appropriate state budgetary support and maintaining its independence from political involvements."

The new difficulty of recruiting new faculty was matched by a pattern of departures from university and college faculties. Ralph Prater, president of San Fernando Valley State College, said at one point in the crisis: "What disturbs me most is that we are losing senior people for the first time. We're losing associate and full professors and even chairmen of departments."

Reagan found new ways to wage his war on the academic community and to discourage faculty, administrators, and students. He was not only stingy on faculty salaries—sometimes vetoing legislation for promised pay raises—but also stepped perilously close to outright political control of professors on philosophical grounds.

In the spring of 1969, Reagan supported and pushed a proposal to diminish academic independence by giving the Regents veto power over the hiring and firing of professors. In February, a controversy developed over the rehiring at the University's San Diego campus of Dr. Herbert Marcuse, a noted Marxist philosopher and writer. In his press conference of February 25, 1969, Reagan was asked about the issue and slithered through a series of semantic evasions obscuring his basic attitude:

QUESTION: "Governor, at the Regents' meeting there was a motion made to censure Dr. McGill [chancellor] in San Diego for his action in hiring Marcuse. How did you vote on that?"

REAGAN: "No, there was no move to censure. . . . We were helpless, there was nothing we could do to alter the situation with regard to Professor Marcuse—his rehiring was an accomplished fact. The Regents then voted to release a statement to the press expressing their displeasure . . . that simply stated that a substantial number of Regents disapproved of the action in the rehiring of Professor Marcuse. . . . A substantial number must have meant majority because it took a majority vote to approve that press statement. I voted for that press statement. . . ."

QUESTION: "Does the Regents' action pretty well guarantee that [Marcuse's] contract will not be renewed next year?"

REAGAN: "What can happen in a year to change someone's mind—you'd have to speak to each individual. I cannot foresee anything that would change my own opinion . . . as to whether he should be there or not."

QUESTION: "Could the Chancellor rehire him without going through the Regents?"

REAGAN: "I have a hunch the Regents will be a little more alert. As a matter of fact, we now have a motion that will be taken up at the next meeting to take the authority of chancellors to make those decisions . . . away from them and return to the Regents the right to approve."

QUESTION: "Would you support such a motion?"

REAGAN: "Yes, I will."

QUESTION: "What are your reasons for your vote on the [previous] Regents' action?"

REAGAN: ". . . I believe there is an imbalance in the faculty of the university system, and frankly I don't believe —this isn't just a case of deciding someone's philosophy or something. I do believe that he [Marcuse] is an open advocate of the type of revolution that's causing so much disturbance in the campuses."

The Governor then complained that some "radical" professors were not just teaching but were also "indoctrinating" students. He left no doubt that he wanted to correct the "philosophical imbalance" by giving the Regents veto power over hiring and firing of professors. The Regents, becoming more conservative with Reagan's votes and influence, at a subsequent meeting approved the motion to assume power of approval over faculty appointments. At his next press conference following that decision, Reagan was asked about the meaning of the new policy and also to expand his complaints about the philosophical imbalance in the faculties. In that context, he launched into a long and lurid narrative about campus disorder, with graphic and grisly phrases about

vandalism, bombs, murders, arson, and beatings. In that
passionate outburst at his press conference of March 25,
1969, Reagan said, "All of this so far has stemmed from the
activities of the far left, or the left, the new left, and I have
yet to see any instances of this having been instigated by
so-called right-wing forces." When asked to comment on one
chancellor's criticism of the Regents' hiring-firing decision,
Reagan dismissed it contemptuously as a "propaganda campaign."

On April 22, Reagan was bluntly asked this question:

QUESTION: "Governor, on the subject of the Board of Regents taking over the hiring at the University of California
. . . you say political philosophy will not enter into the
decision. What other than political philosophy are the Regents competent to judge a man by as to whether he should
or shouldn't teach?"

REAGAN: "This question has come up before as to whether
the Regents are competent to make these decisions or not,
and I challenge the assumption that in the whole United
States and in all of government and everything the only
facet of government that should be allowed to run itself
without any public control whatsoever is in the educational
field. . . ."

QUESTION: ". . . Mr. [William] Roth, who is one of the
Regents, said he's never known of any instance where a Regent has considered a faculty appointment that hasn't been
on a political basis. . . ."

REAGAN: ". . . Mr. Roth is distorting the situation. . . . I
never heard of anyone on our side . . . opposed to a faculty
member bring up his politics as a reason."

QUESTION: " Well, could you explain then, Governor, you
once talked about the controversy over Professor Marcuse
. . . and you've said he represented a political imbalance in
the system. . . ."

REAGAN: "He's in one of the inexact sciences, philosophy, to be exact, and the thing . . . is not so much the views of an individual as the lack of competency when an individual reveals that he injects his own views in his teaching. . . ."

In July, 1968, education writer William Trombley, in *The Los Angeles Times,* offered a fascinating comparison of higher education in the states of California and New York. He noted that New York State, previous to Nelson Rockefeller's election in 1958, had a tradition of private universities and colleges, and that California, before Reagan's election, "had the finest system of public higher education in the country." Trombley continued:

"Rockefeller decided that New York State must have a quality public higher educational system, whatever the cost, in order to prosper in the last half of the twentieth century.

"Reagan decided that the cost of California higher education must be reduced, even if it meant loss of leadership in a field that has always been regarded as crucial to the state's economic growth and social well-being.

"In every area of higher education development the figures point up a startling contrast between the policies of the two governors.

"The Rockefeller Administration has spent $1 billion on new higher education construction in the last six years. Another $2 billion will be spent by 1975.

"But in California the Reagan Administration has reduced UC and state college construction requests by about 50 per cent. . . .

"In New York, new university campuses have been built at Albany, Binghamton, and Stony Brook. . . .

"But, in California, plans for new UC campuses in northern and southern California have been shelved. . . .

"Compounding the problem, Governor Reagan has refused to support a new bond issue for higher education construction, badly needed if the university and the state colleges are to keep up with expanding enrollments. . . ."

Inevitably—with Reagan's antitaxes, antispending, antieducation phrases ringing in their ears—California voters turned down that $250 million bond issue for construction and health services on the campuses.

The Governor's war against higher education sunk to a low and despicable level when Robert F. Kennedy was assassinated in Los Angeles in June, 1968. In a letter to college Trustees and university Regents, mailed the day after the Senator's death, Reagan linked the murder to "today's climate of violence."

"A sick campus community in California in many ways is responsible for a sick community around these campuses," Reagan wrote. His letter, made public, continued:

"It is time for [Trustees and Regents] to reassess their own goals, their pattern of only reacting to crisis, meeting by meeting, and the degree to which they have delegated away responsibility and abandoned principle."

The letter questioned "constant resistance" by some professors and administrators to "the rightful place of law enforcement in a democratic society," then concluded:

"Do you think that constant appeasement of those who coerce . . . is likely to strengthen confidence in society, in leadership, in fair play?"

Reagan's sense of "fair play" in relation to the university Regents seemed to vary, depending on whether or not they agreed with him. He was publicly pleased about the Regents and defended their "competence" when they voted with him on the issue of veto power over hiring and firing of faculty. But when the Regents turned down, by 13 to 8, a motion by Reagan to sweep away such faculty prerogatives as establishment and supervision of courses, the Governor blew up. On October 21, 1968, he accused the Regents of "disdain and deliberate unconcern for the interests of the people."

The Governor's anti-education policies toward public schools below the university and college level have been only slightly less destructive than his war on higher education. In early 1968, Milton L. Schwartz, outgoing Vice President of the State Board of Education, said, in a farewell statement, that Reagan was "the greatest destructive force and enemy of public education in fifty years." Schwartz—a Republican —said that 1967 was "a black, black page in the history of public education. In previous years, we made progress, but last year public education moved at a dizzy pace in a backward direction." He listed these actions on various school measures:

• A bill to provide funds to train teachers of disadvantaged children—cut one-third by Reagan.

• A bill to help gifted children of disadvantaged families —vetoed by Reagan.

• A bill to provide college education grants to poverty area children—vetoed by Reagan.

• A bill to raise the minimum salaries of teachers in California to $6,000 a year—vetoed by Reagan.

Schwartz was angry, a typical reaction to Reagan's negative policies and actions on education. "You can't justify these things on the grounds of fiscal responsibility and economy," the education leader said. "These measures and others like them were passed by the legislature. But the Governor is willing to sign a bill giving property tax relief of $5 million to oil companies."

There were a few brief moments in early 1970 when Reagan seemed ready to de-escalate his war against the campus. In his "State of the State" address to the legislature in January, he refrained—for the first time in four years—from attacking campus militants. He gave only a light tap to the wrists of youth for "excessive action" and instead called on youth to join with him in a "meaningful involvement . . . at the heart of the Creative Society."

Two months later, the Governor was in a different mood. On his first campaign swing after announcing his candidacy for re-election, Reagan was heckled and picketed by students in Chico, San Bernardino, Eureka, San Jose, and Santa Barbara. On March 17, in Redding, he shook his fists at the abusive hecklers and later raged, "I'm not going to be driven into hiding . . . by any kind of spoiled brats." The next day, in Santa Barbara while another group of students chanted outside a restaurant in which he was speaking, the Governor announced another "crackdown." He told guests at the $25-a-plate Republican luncheon that he would ask the university Regents to adopt a resolution *requiring* the chancellors to suspend student and faculty "troublemakers" during periods of campus disorder. The turmoil, he added, "has severely tarnished the image of the university [and] has endangered the passage of proposition 1 on the June ballot to provide needed funds to expand the university's schools of medicine."

The other fleeting hint of a change of heart in the Reagan war against higher education came in a statement in March by the Governor's Finance Director, Verne Orr. At the beginning of a speech to the California Taxpayers Association in San Francisco, the Reagan Finance Director blithely boasted about how the university and college budgets had *increased* in four years, and proclaimed: "There is not one area in which the Reagan Administration has been more fair, generous, and liberal than in higher education." (I'm glad I wasn't there; I either would have burst out laughing or would have fallen out of my chair.) Orr's perverted claim of charity toward higher education, of course, was based on the misleading, narrow fact that the budget had increased—it was bound to because of rising enrollments and inflation. He did not mention that, a month before, Reagan had chopped the university Regents budget request by $41 million.

However shallow the pretense of charity toward higher education, it only lasted a moment. Before Orr's speech was over, he was attacking college and university administrators for their complaints about budget slashes, charging that they "are failing to turn out a saleable product" and warning ominously that the higher education system might "have to find new administrators."

In his 1970 "State of the State" message to the legislature, Reagan almost soared with eloquence as he challenged California's government leaders to "be more concerned with the next generation than the next election."

It was the beginning of an election year. I could not help wondering and worrying about what kind of concern Reagan would show during 1970 for "the next generation"—which includes and will be led by the students of the universities and colleges. I could not help wondering how much the deep cuts in the university budget in California would affect the next generation, and how much they would affect the decisions of tax-conscious voters in the elections months away. And I couldn't help wondering whether those voters—in November—would more clearly remember Reagan's noble rhetoric or the televised image of his clenched fists and his rage at the "spoiled brats."

10

The Politics of Life

In January, 1970, Governor Reagan devoted one-third of the time and content of his "State of the State" legislative address to the subject of conservation and environment control.

His budget message of the same month called for spending exactly one dollar out of each $516 of state funds for conservation and environment control.

In politics and government, it's the moment-of-truth budget decisions that separate the men from the boys. On the vital and now stylish issue of environment control and ecology, Reagan is boyish to his bones. He is appropriately eloquent now on the subject of pollution, resources control, and the preservation of the world's natural values and beauty. But, as usual, his economy ax clearly cuts through the promises.

Someone on Reagan's speech-writing staff must have a

sincere and perceptive commitment on the issue of conservation and ecology. The State of the State message by the Governor issued this appropriate challenge:

"A booming economy and the 'good life' will be no good at all if our air is too dirty to breathe, our water too polluted to use, our surroundings too noisy, and our land too cluttered and littered to allow us to live decently."

Despite that grand-sounding commitment by the Governor, there is no indication that Reagan is moving on the vital steps toward the salvation of California's magnificent natural resources and beauties. He does deserve credit for his water quality control efforts, but that's about all.

Even in his State of the State address, Reagan equivocated on some of the pressing problems of environment control. He said that he was for a ban on new drilling for oil in offshore areas of California under the jurisdiction of the state. But he said nothing about *halting* the continuing drilling of several rigs that were, at that moment, leaking oil into the ocean and onto the beaches of Santa Barbara. And, for the previous year and a half, during which the offshore oil drilling was fouling the beaches and killing wildlife, Reagan had been characteristically evasive.

Reagan's State of the State address subtly acknowledged his sympathies for the corporate interest above the broader public interest on the environment issue.

"Progress and preservation are compatible," he said in a well-cadenced and alliterative phrase. "It is the refusal to work together for the proper balance that is incompatible with the spirit of the seventies."

What that means—when one looks at the budget and other more specific statements of Reagan—is that he doesn't think the state government ought to interfere with corporations that, while making their products and profits, foul the waters, air, and lands of California.

Reagan, as a politician in an election year, knows and senses when a public mood is shifting toward demands for action on some issue in which the government ought to exert leadership. In 1969 and 1970, Californians became worried, demanding, and vocal on the issue of conservation and ecology. So Reagan, in his State of the State address and other general pronouncements, offered a firm-sounding promise of action. But, in terms of commitment and budget, he has done little.

Example: One of his proposals in the State of the State message called for a program of conservation education in California schools—to inform students and future citizens of the need to preserve the diminishing resources of the state. A few years before, the legislature had approved a bill for conservation education; Reagan vetoed it. In 1967, he did sign a similar bill, but the funds to finance the program were killed when his Finance Director opposed them in legislative hearings.

Reagan, in numerous statements in 1969 and 1970, boasted that California had adopted, during his administration, the "toughest" antismog measure. In fact, that legislation became law because of the leadership and initiative of several state legislators—Democrats and Republicans—without Reagan lifting a finger to help it along.

On two other environment measures—to protect the beautiful Lake Tahoe in California's Sierra Mountains and the magnificent San Francisco Bay—Reagan pretended, in his State of the State message, that he was the savior of those two valued water bodies. The truth is that, while several state legislators were fighting hard against vested interests that were polluting Lake Tahoe and filling in San Francisco Bay, Reagan did and said nothing.

Some informed observers saw through Reagan's rhetoric in early 1970. C. K. McClatchy, executive editor of the *Sacramento Bee*, wrote in one column:

"Would you believe Governor Reagan, the brave conservationist, bucking the powerful oil interests to save the flora and fauna? Well, get ready, because that is the script for 1970. . . .

"The public has felt the sting of smog from San Diego to the upper Sacramento Valley and it does not feel good. Nor does the public like the idea of living surrounded by polluted lakes, streams, rivers, and bays, which are of little worth for fishing or swimming.

"The real question—can a politician who for four years actively opposed many important conservation measures pass himself off as a candidate who now believes in all the things he refused to support in the past?"

That question is not just abstractly political. Reagan's budget-cutting priority had a negative effect on conservation and environment-preservation efforts long before ecology became a major public issue.

The Calavaras Big Trees State Park in California's magnificent Sierra Mountains represents the stark contrast between the policies and budgets of previous state administrations and those of Reagan's. The North Grove of the park, developed in the mid-1950's, offers the people the chance to enjoy and be a part of the beautiful setting with a minimum disruption of nature. In the North Grove are all-weather walkways meandering unobtrusively through the forest, spacious campsites, clean and modern rest-room and washing facilities, and scenic roadways.

One gently winding roadway leads to the South Grove of the park, an equally magnificent natural area, which was opened to visitors and dedicated in mid-1969. Originally, the State Parks budget reserved about $1 million for development of the South Grove. Reagan slashed that item to $400,-000.

The results, in comparison with the North Grove, are obvious. The scenic roadway into the South Grove abruptly narrows to a poorly graded slice through the trees, and for one 300 foot stretch, it can accommodate only one-way traffic. When the South Grove was dedicated, Reagan's Director of Parks and Recreation said the road was designed "to slow people down" so "they will take time to look at and appreciate the beautiful vistas." The road, in fact, was designed by park personnel themselves because there were no funds for State Division of Highways engineers to draw the plans. And park employees did most of the construction work themselves because of lack of funds for a more professional effort.

In the South Grove, the facilities for picnickers and campers are meager—no ovens and, instead of permanent restroom facilities, only a few rented, portable toilets. The hiking trail in the South Grove—much of it carved by park personnel in their spare time—wanders crudely through areas of loose dirt; in some spots, it is kicked up into dust clouds by hikers' feet. The hiking trails in the North Grove are covered with wood chips.

Other drastic changes have been made in California's state park system. In early 1967, Reagan announced a new plan under which some parks would be developed and operated by private concessioners instead of with state funds. His plan called for moves toward a "pay-as-you-go" system—including a big increase in admission fees to parks throughout the state. Under the guise of relieving the taxpayer, that really meant that nature-lovers and campers would have to pay more to enjoy the publicly owned parks and that private businesses would profit from the operation.

In the long and controversial effort to establish a Redwoods National Park in California, Reagan pretended to be a strong supporter of a big national preserve of the magnificent trees along California's North Coast area. In fact, his antifederal attitudes and commercial orientation delayed and often confused the struggle to establish the park.

"I believe our country can and should have a Redwood National Park in California," he said to a U.S. Senate Interior Subcommittee hearing in 1967. But, the next day, in Sacramento, he said: "There can be no proof given that a national park is necessary to preserve the redwoods. The State of California has already maintained a great conservation program."

The Governor was slow to support a compromise, sponsored by Senator Thomas H. Kuchel, between the demands of the conservationist Sierra Club and the meager offerings of the lumber industry on the acreage for the park. He bluntly told a congressional committee that he was determined to drive a hard bargain in exchange for allowing two state park areas to be included in the National Park—demanding turnover of certain other federally owned lands to the state. He seemed to ignore the fact that the federal government was willing to invest tens of millions of dollars in a park of benefit to Californians as well as visitors to the state. After Reagan's demands were expressed, the chairman of the House Interior Subcommitee hearing the issue noted, "California should be less demanding. It certainly would speed up things and get us closer to a favorable solution."

In his press conference of July 11, 1967, Reagan also acknowledged that one big barrier to the establishment of the National Redwoods Park was his insistence for additional "protection" for private timber interests. On that date, Reagan was asked directly whether or not officials of the lumber company involved, Rellim-Miller, had contributed to his election campaign. Reagan said he didn't know. But his executive secretary later confirmed that Darrell Schroeder, general manager of the firm, had been Reagan's campaign finance chairman in a northern county the previous year.

On another key environment issue—smog—*San Francisco*

Chronicle columnist Charles McCabe put down Reagan's conservationist pretensions with these biting comments:

"It is the mark of the successful politician that he faces the inevitable, and then takes credit for it.

"Jumping on the bandwagon can be made to look like leadership if the move is made dexterously enough.

"Which is precisely what our dexterous Governor in Sacramento is presently trying to do with smog, which he has discovered is a hot political issue.

"It is a hot political issue because, among other reasons, physicians in one recent year advised 15,000 of their patients to move [because of] emphysema, chronic bronchitis, and asthma.

"Governor Reagan . . . recently unleashed a six-point program against smog. Its major provision would convert many of the state government's 25,000 motor vehicles to dual low-emission natural gas and gasoline fuel systems.

"As might be expected, the Governor came around too late and with far to little.

"Furthermore, he tried to kidnap the smog issue from the man who has really been doing something about it in this state—a Democratic Senator from Oakland named Nicholas C. Petris."

Senator Petris had worked diligently for years on the smog crisis in California. He even succeeded in winning State Senate approval for his bill to ban the sale of internal combustion engine cars in California starting in 1975, a necessarily drastic measure, which died in the State Assembly.

There are times when drastic steps are necessary by the government for the preservation of life. In the 1950's and 1960's, California's government had foresight and took some drastic steps to produce a monumental, life-saving program, which is now nearing completion: the California Water Project. No such foresight can be found in the Reagan Administration.

The California Water Project is one of the biggest—if not *the* biggest—construction programs in the history of man. Its purposes are varied, but the central, massive goal was based on a single fact evident to state engineers and leaders in the early 1950's: More than 70 per cent of California's water originates in the northern one-third of the state; 77 per cent of the water needs are in the southern two-thirds of the state.

Another stark fact challenged state officials in the early 1950's: Most rain and subsequent river run-off in California come in the winter and the spring; the greatest demand for water is in the summer.

The goal—to capture water in the times and places of its source and transport it to the places of need at the right time —required a big commitment by engineers and public leaders during my administrations and those of my predecessors, Earl Warren and Goodwin J. Knight. It also required billions of dollars of funds. The first stages of the project were authorized in 1951 under Governor Warren, the first state appropriation for it came under Governor Knight in 1957, and the full commitment for the billions necessary was exercised during my first administration in 1959 and the early 1960's.

The California Water Project was the most important single project during my terms as Governor—and the most controversial. The huge financial investment aroused passionate opposition by frugal, tax-conscious groups in the state. Regional jealousies and rivalries were aroused; many northern Californians were furious about spending all that money "to send our water down to fill up those swimming pools in Los Angeles." Some powerful voices in the state attacked me as I had never been attacked before or since. *The San Francisco Chronicle*, in editorials and cartoons, depicted me as a bumbling ogre who had created a greedy octopus (the water project), which was strangling the north.

The battles—engineering, fiscal, legislative, and political —were fought and won. Some of the controversy still continues in the state, but the California Water Project is nearing completion as a source of life for thousands of acres of dry land and millions of people. There are other vital byproducts of the project, including recreation and flood control. In 1964, for example, portions of the project that had been completed were credited with averting a Sacramento Valley flood potentially worse than a 1955 disaster, which killed thirty-six people and destroyed 400 homes in Yuba City. What greater service can government provide to society than the saving of human lives? The firm knowledge that the California Water Project had saved lives easily counterbalanced, for me, as Governor, all the work, the budget battles, and the stinging personal and political pains of the attacks against me.

In May, 1968, a key part of the California Water Project —the Oroville Dam—was dedicated. It rose higher than any other earth-fill dam in the world: 770 feet. Its 80 million cubic yards of earth and rock were ten times the mass of Egypt's pyramids. At its top, it stretched across a distance twice as long as the Golden Gate Bridge. All of those facts were awesome, but what truly moved me was that the Oroville Dam, even when it was only partially constructed, saved the lives of human beings in 1964 and would help send life-giving water to many crowded or lifeless areas of the state in future years.

Reagan, as Governor in 1968, led the dedication ceremonies at the Oroville Dam. He appropriately did not seek to share any credit for the achievement, and he did praise "the vision, the dedication, and the hard work" of many Californians for the California Water Project. But Reagan's prominent role at the dedication was ironic. The California Water Project was developed through the types of governmental effort that Reagan so militantly avoids: expenditures of billions of dollars, cooperation with the federal government, detailed planning for the distant future, a trust in technical experts and engineers, and conciliation between conflicting social groups (in this case, north vs. south).

California is naturally blessed not only with resources that —if properly harnessed and used—can sustain and preserve life for tens of millions of people. The state is also graced by natural beauties that can enhance and improve the quality of life and living for the people.

I learned to love the beauties of California early and never lost my keen appreciation for them. I was born in San Francisco, a city that rests in what must be the loveliest physical setting of any city in the world. As a boy, I spent my summers at my grandparents' farm in Colusa County, riding horseback over the beautiful hills and sharing the chores of farm life. When I was a teenager, my father drove the family to Lake Tahoe and Yosemite and I viewed the grandeur of the Sierras for the first time. To this day—half a century later—I recall vividly the pleasure and awe of first seeing Yosemite Valley from Glacier Point. My wife and I returned to that spot a few years ago. I was just as excited and exultant in the beauty of the scene as I'd been as a teenager.

Even as Governor, when there was so little personal time away from the constant demands of the office, I was determined to remain aware of the unique natural beauties of California. At least once a year, I trekked into one of California's many unspoiled, wilderness areas for a full week or more. My state forestry, fish and game, and other conservation officials came along, sometimes with their federal counterparts. We went into indescribably beautiful, untouched areas on horseback, camping out and not seeing a vestige of man's society. We slept under the stars, ate under the sky, and tramped the trails of the high Sierra, the Marble Mountains, and the Trinity Alps. The air in those far mountain wilderness areas was clear, the water in the fast-running streams pure. I can recall turning to Hugo Fisher, the head of the State Resources Agency, and saying, in essence: "What a great job you have! You are the trustee, the conservator for a time, of the true values of this great state we have inherited."

I believe that we are serving God when we appreciate the gifts of nature that are passed to us. And we serve better when we seek to protect and preserve the beauties of the earth for others to see and appreciate.

Politics, to me, is not just the battle for power, the formation of policy, the struggles for budgets, the waging of election campaigns. The essence and central goal of politics and political government, in my view, is to protect life and to improve the quality of living for the people of a society. As Governor of California, I not only struggled to keep the society from being overwhelmed by the problems of a skyrocketing rise in population, to keep pace with the needs of the people for the services of government. I also wanted their government to help make life a bit more pleasant for them and to diminish some of the distressing aspects of life in a modern, complex society.

A government centered on the politics of life has difficult choices to make, and sometimes the consequences of those choices cannot be known firmly in advance. The need for highways and freeways offers an example of the dilemma. As Governor, I did not want the ever-rising demands for more and bigger freeways to go unmet. That would mean that the lives of millions of Californians would be complicated and diminished by the frustrating, time-consuming confinement to jammed, overcrowded freeways during the commuter hours in urban areas. For the past few decades, more people have meant more cars—and a rising need for sufficient roadways to transport them. A man who had to spend three hours a day inching along in bumper-to-bumper traffic to get to and from work lived a flawed life. So I pushed hard for more and better freeways to ease the life-reducing effects of an obsolete freeway system in California. We built new, bigger, and wider freeways to give millions of Californians more time to be themselves and to be with their families outside the hours of work.

But freeways have adverse effects. They slash through lands that are needed for other purposes and they provide a compacted outlet for the production of more cars, which send more pollutants into the air. The resulting poisonous smog endangers the health and lives of the people of our cities.

The politics of life—government that seeks to enhance living and to protect human life—thus involves intrinsic conflicts that are difficult to resolve. In the attempt to simplify and enhance the daily lives of the human beings who commute into and around our cities, shouldn't we build more freeways? And, in the attempt to reduce smog and save the lungs and lives of the people in and around our cities, shouldn't we discourage the use of cars by *stopping* freeway construction? There is no easy answer. But, clearly, drastic steps are needed today to find the answer—perhaps including the bill by State Senator Petris to ban the internal combustion engine in automobiles, which might force manufacturers to come up with a nontoxic method for transporting people or stimulate development of rapid transit systems. (In the early 1960's, I pushed a bill through the legislature, which paved the way to passage of a bond issue for the Bay Area Rapid Transit system. Reagan has said in press conferences that he "hasn't thought much" about rapid transit.)

A state park system is another example of the dilemma. It is, in one sense, sad to cut a roadway, hiking trails, and campsites into a magnificent grove of redwoods, which stands in pure beauty as a gift of God. But human beings need a chance to observe and appreciate that beauty, so the roadways and other facilities must be built. For all my love of the untouched wilderness areas of California, I do not believe that the beauties of this state should be regarded as some sort of holy shrine to be removed from the enjoyment of human beings. The answer on this issue is the careful, costly, nature-respecting effort to achieve a delicate balance between preserving the beauty and opening it to the human senses. Some lovely areas of the state should be opened to the people with careful—and costly—park development. But other beautiful regions should be preserved as wilderness areas, with absolute bans on construction of roadways or other facilities.

Though the politics of life presents difficult dilemmas, the modern political leader cannot remain indecisive. Life moves on, and in California it moves on at a dizzying pace, which requires immediate choices and decisions. Government makes those choices, by action or inaction.

But government cannot play God. The most urgent pleas of the extremist ecologists today call for the government to take authoritative steps to reduce the population. They ask not just for the dissemination of birth control information to the people, but for extreme laws that would discourage or ban any more than two children per family. There is no question that there is an immediate crisis of environment and ecology today, particularly in California. Raymond F. Dasmann brilliantly outlined the truth of the crisis in his excellent, ahead-of-the-times book *The Destruction of California*, published in 1965. After defining the crisis, Dasmann suggested basically that California should control the population increase "by not providing for it . . . indeed forbidding the development of new facilities." That *may* be the answer to the environment crisis. But, in the meantime, government must provide the basic services that the lives of its people require.

Other ecologists have suggested that if society and life in any one area becomes "repulsive" enough, the people will stop regenerating or will stay away from the particular area —and then survival will be possible. For all my philosophical instincts favoring strong, central leadership of society in government, I believe that a contrived attempt to make life "repulsive" in a society in order to save it is dangerously presumptuous.

Unintentionally, I'm sure, Ronald Reagan has embarked on a policy, which is allied with the proposals of some of the more extremist ecologists who are usually critical of his detailed decisions. They want a society that simply does not provide the services and facilities that will accommodate more people, thus "discouraging" more people, more cars, more pollution, more destruction. Reagan's budgets and programs may just do that. By curtailing opportunities for education and cutting every service from freeways to mental health to state park facilities, he could make California so crowded, confused, and unattractive that people will stop moving into the state. In any extended period of the Reagan policy and program, California—the beautiful golden land of opportunity and hope—would become a repulsive place in which to live.

I, too, care about the survival of future generations, who will need unpolluted air, water, and land in order to live at all. But, as a moderate politician who knows that government must play a limited role in influencing the course of life for mankind, I resist the politics of repulsion. A Governor of California is responsible to the people who are living now. His decisions should not harm or diminish their lives on the vague and questionable hope that Californians of tomorrow will survive because life here is more unpleasant and repulsive.

The trouble with Reagan, I feel, is that he does not consider these possible consequences of his actions as Governor. I doubt that he looks very far ahead or wonders about the results when he cuts a budget or kills a program that benefits the lives of people now. Reagan is fond of saying that he does not believe in "tampering with the natural rhythms of life." The worried ecologists use almost the same words. But what Reagan means is that government should not interfere with an abstract economic process involving the free-flowing activities of something he calls "the private sector." It doesn't seem to bother Reagan that the "rhythms of life" are being tampered with when lumber firms chop down priceless groves of 2,000 year-old-redwood trees or the offshore wells of private oil companies foul the water, beaches, wildlife, and beauty of California's coast.

Personally and politically, Reagan appears to believe that corporate profit is the great motivating force for the solution of society's problems and the progress of man. He obviously believes that the great enemy of man and the good life is the monolithic monster of government.

11

Reagan the Reactionary Radical

A few years ago, a Yale University economist conducted a unique study to determine how the "quality of life" varied in the different states and regions of the nation. Dr. John O. Wilson admitted the difficulty of measuring the quality of life, but he confidently used an original and careful method called the Social-Economic-Political Index. The index was based on eight domestic goals defined by a Commission on National Goals appointed by President Eisenhower in 1960. After measuring each state with the SEP index of national goals, Dr. Wilson listed them in order of excellence from one of fifty.

"The results of the rankings," he wrote, "showed that California provides the highest composite level of quality of life in the nation, followed by Minnesota, Connecticut, Massachusetts, and Washington."

The survey based on the criteria of President Eisenhower's Commission was conducted *before* the negative policies and programs of Governor Reagan began to diminish the quality of life in California.

The obvious paradox today is that the man who took over as Governor of the state with the best "quality of life" possesses a philosophy and record that are almost antithetical to the spirit of the domestic goals defined by President Eisenhower's Commission.

It is interesting to think back to Reagan's pronouncements and actions as Governor in the context of the eight goals, which helped determine California's unsurpassed ranking in the nation. I list those goals here, with my own nonscientific but thoughtful grading of Reagan on each;

1. *"Status of the Individual*—enhancing personal dignity, promoting maximum development of capabilities, and widening the opportunities for individual choice." (Giving Reagan an immense benefit of doubt. I grade him with a C– here—but only because of his rhetorical emphasis on the supremacy of the individual.)

2. *"Democratic Process*—building an informed and involved citizenry, improving the quality of public administration, and increasing collaboration and the sharing of power among all levels of government." (He gets a charitable D, only because more power—and responsibility—has fallen to local governments.)

3. *"Education*—improving the quality and quantity of primary, secondary, higher, and vocational education and training." (An emphatic F!)

4. *"Economic Growth*—increasing both the quantity and quality of growth, including capital investment in the public sector, improved standard of living, and training for a more capable and flexible work force." (Another F; Reagan has preached and practiced *cutback*, not growth.)

5. *"Technological Change—*increasing the effort in research and the availability of manpower and facilities to maintain economic growth and improve living conditions." (I grade him with a D– in this category, only because he could do nothing to stop the vast technological research effort by private institutions in the state.)

6. *"Agriculture—*seeking an efficient sized farm sector with a fair return to the farmer; helping excess agriculture workers relocate in more productive areas." (Reagan wins a C grade in the first half of that category, an F in the second.)

7. *"Living Conditions—*the alleviation of general poverty and the decayed conditions in our cities." (An unqualified F.)

8. *"Health and Welfare"—*improving the level of welfare asistance, effort in vocational rehabilitation, and provision of medical services in both the public and private sectors of our economy." (A very big F.)

Totaling up Reagan's grades on the criteria of the President's Commission on National Goals, the Governor flunks. If there were a college of public service training to boost the quality of life for the people, I doubt that Reagan would get through the first freshman semester.

His most glaring failure is in the category that Dr. Wilson considered the most crucial. The economist wrote:

"If one area could be singled out for the importance of its impact on the total quality of life, *education* would probably be selected. The quantity and quality of education influence three other goal areas: individual status, economic growth, and technological change."

The grading of Reagan I have offered above is not intended to be facetious. It is one attempt to dramatize the radical difference between Reagan's governmental policies and the basic values and goals that had come to be accepted in American society.

California's superb "Quality of Life,' I believe, is threatened by the Reagan Administration. I have no doubt that the state would drop far below the first-rank standing if Dr. Wilson conducted a similar survey following many more years of Reagan rule.

Generally, Reagan tends to think of himself, and is labeled, as a "conservative" politically. His critics, Democrats and Republicans, often call him a "reactionary." In my view of his deeds and words, those labels are too mild. Reagan is a radical. Not only do his views depart radically from such conventional values and goals as defined by President Eisenhower's Commission, but his performance as Governor represents a radical shift away from a pattern of moderately progressive leadership running through the history of California in this century. Under Reagan, California's government has taken a 180-degree turn away from the social, political, and economic directions dating back to the administrations of Hiram Johnson in the first decade of the twentieth century.

The essence of that progressive tradition is that a free people can and should use their representative government as a tool to advance and enhance their lives. For six decades, California moved in the direction of pragmatic, humanitarian reform. There was no carte blanche for unchecked central government; Governor (and, later, Senator) Hiram Johnson established laws and precedents that assured a high degree of responsiveness by state government to the people and a low incidence of political corruption in Sacramento. But the essential value and assumption was that government should be a positive channel for collective, public progress.

The progressive political pattern continued, with few interruptions, through the administrations of Earl Warren and to the end of my second administration in 1966. Governor Warren, in particular, carried the progressive California pattern to a high point of excellence by pioneering ventures into new social areas. California during his terms was *ahead* of the national government with such programs as disability insurance for workers and medical care for the elderly. Before my election in 1958, the state had had only one Democratic Governor. But the moderate-progressive leadership extended from Hiram Johnson through a dozen Republican Governors, with only one significant exception.

That exception was Friend W. Richardson, elected in 1922 but defeated for re-election in 1926. Richardson, a big, energetic and tough-minded Quaker, traveled more than 50,000 miles by car in his 1922 campaign and profited both from the new campaign mobility and a conservative tide, which was sweeping the country following World War I. There are striking similarities between the term of Richardson starting in 1923 and Reagan's starting in 1967. Reporter and California historian Herbert L. Phillips described Richardson's administration as "a time of reprisal" against the progressive forces established under Hiram Johnson, and added:

"Almost at once in the 1923 legislature came concerted efforts under the Richardson Administration toward wholesale budget trimming, an erosion of the state's business regulatory operations, a harassment of education, and appropriation cutbacks for what Johnson had called 'humanitarian functions.' "

The description would be apt for Reagan's Administration in the late 1960's, but the similarity of Richardson and Reagan ends there. Richardson, often bull headed and heavy handed, failed to break the progressive pattern of government in California. The influence of the Governor in that period was substantially less than now, when the mass media and television carry the face and voice of a leader instantly to the vast majority of the people. And Richardson was not too far removed, in time, from an earlier century of Old West values, which placed government low on the scale of public esteem. He lasted only four years and remained the major exception to the strengthening progressive tradition in California's society.

A sense of history and an awareness of Richardson's reactionary term do not assuage my concern—pained concern—for the radicalism of Reagan as Governor. Events move more swiftly today than in the 1920's. Society is changing as quickly as electronic images move from Sacramento to every home in the state. The decisions of government today affect far more lives than in the earlier decades of the century. On basic issues of survival—society's and man's—there is less time for the public wisdom to become coherent and reflect itself politically. For all the checks and counterbalances on a Governor's formal authority, he is an immensely powerful force in modern California.

Reagan has used this power and force to challenge, cut back, or scuttle policies and programs that developed during the sixty years of progressive California leadership. Many of the specific projects begun by Governor Warren (whom Reagan disparaged often while he was Chief Justice of the United States) are now diminished or threatened entirely by the present Governor, not to mention efforts that I initiated. But the most pronounced feature of Reagan's radicalism is the extreme effect he has in tarnishing the respect of the people for their government. The whole concept of government as a positive extension of the will of a free people is being more deeply undermined by Reagan in California today.

Almost four years in the Governor's office have not basically modified Reagan's antigovernment attitude, which is radically in excess of the normal citizen's careful skepticism of bureaucracy. On March 10, 1970, when he announced his candidacy for re-election, Reagan sounded the same simple, negative themes of his campaign of 1966. He would, he said, promote individualism and let Californians progress with "little interference" from Sacramento. He promised each citizen that he would "get the government off your back." He said that the 1970's "can bring a whole new dimension to California if we recognize the spirit which started this nation in 1776."

Reagan fails to recognize that the spirit of 1776 was aimed toward the establishment of a representative, democratic government. The founding fathers—in a *revolutionary* spirit, which Reagan also chooses to ignore—were against King George III, not against government.

In his attacks on the whole concept of government, Reagan seldom suggests any positive alternative—except for indecipherable pleas for "a whole new dimension" or vague references to the ill-defined deity he calls the "private sector." Even after several years in which he has presumably faced the realities of society in the Governor's office, Reagan seems to think that business, industry, and private individuals will eagerly rush in to help provide those services and fulfill those responsibilities that his administration abandons. Unfortunately, there was no rush by the "private sector" to provide emergency dental care for impoverished children or school lunches for hungry children when Reagan cut those programs out of the budget.

It is obvious to me that Reagan just doesn't like government. It is the political paradox of contemporary California that such a man occupies the highest office of state government. That makes about as much sense to me as placing a church under the supervision of an atheist.

That comparison is not meant to suggest that I believe government is sacred, above criticism or reform. Nor do I think that a political pattern or tradition is perfect or worthy just because it has endured for a long time. As a young man, I was deeply impressed by a radio commentary by Raymond Clapper in which he discussed inviolate ideas and ideals. Most people, Clapper said, form an ideal early—in politics or anything else—and then stick it away in a dark closet of the mind as if it were eternally valid. Ideas and ideals, Clapper said (and I agree) should be pulled out and exposed to the light frequently, for re-examination and perhaps revision.

Reagan has no such flexibility of ideas and attitudes, not since he became a convert to radical Republicanism twenty years ago. In his attitude toward government, he is fixed and rigid—seeking with some success to end public respect, confidence, and trust in government but offering no firm alternative. As a politician and public executive, he dismantles instead of constructs, destroys instead of builds.

The negative and destructive features of Reagan's politics are matched by his inability to respect and consider an opposing viewpoint. I have emphasized, in several earlier chapters of this book, that he makes little effort to conciliate between rival groups in society; with instinctively rigid viewpoint, he quickly chooses sides. On issues in which he is publicly and previously committed, he is equally averse to compromise. The spirit of reasonable compromise is perhaps the most significant and deeply ingrained element of American politics and government. The Constitution itself was a child of compromise between conflicting views on the proper role of government. Reagan's extreme reluctance to engage in reasonable conciliation or compromise is another basic and radical departure from the American political tradition.

One of the supreme ironies of Reagan's role today is a sort of unrecognized, *defacto* alliance between him and many of the student radicals he so regularly denounces. On the surface, they are sworn enemies in the turmoil that surrounds campus disorders. But there are deep and pervasive similarities of political radicalism between Reagan and the angrier representatives of what has been described as the youth "counter-culture."

Both Reagan and the more nihilistic student radicals are profoundly antigovernment.

Both are deeply suspicious of the influence of "experts" in this modern technological age.

Both are far more concerned and occupied with the process of tearing down or dismantling existing systems and values than in perfecting and proposing new alternatives.

Both are insistently anti-intellectual, clinging to a few simplistic slogans or platitudes to justify their actions.

Both are rigid, uncompromising, and often emotional in their political conduct.

Both tend strongly to judge others quickly with a "good guys–bad guys" perspective.

Both are skilled in attracting and using television as a means of gaining public attention.

Both are inclined to be overeager in the use of force in a dispute or conflict, not to resolve it but to *win* it.

And—most dangerously for our society—both Reagan and the more radical militants are practitioners of what has come to be called "the politics of confrontation."

Reagan's relaxed, easy-going style in formal public appearances disguises another style, which might be called controlled belligerence. Occasionally, his temper flares publicly, as in Redding in March, 1970, when he clenched his fists and screamed "spoiled brats" at radical, chanting students or, in April, 1970, when he seemed to welcome a campus "bloodbath." But, more often, Reagan seems to plan the belligerent confrontations for political advantage. Reviewing the first three years of the Reagan term in December 28, 1969, *Sacramento Bee* writer Peter Weisser concluded:

"One of the hallmarks of the Reagan administration, in

contrast to Brown's, was the entire politics of on-camera confrontation—rather than accommodation.

"Time and again large delegations, often students, sometimes militants, came to the Capitol. Time and again Reagan met them, waited out the boos, and said his piece.

"And time and again the results were the same—an inflamed crowd, a righteous governor, and an overwhelmingly pro-Reagan reaction from television news viewers, who may or may not have understood the particular issues involved. . . ."

Reagan's political radicalism is of the independent variety; his anti-intellectualism stifles any instinct he might have to develop or adopt a dogmatic organized philosophy. But he is notably more tolerant of far-right-wing attitudes and actions than of the antics of the far left. He seldom speaks out about the militant and even revolutionary right-wing groups—some of which are stockpiling weapons and distributing manuals on guerrilla warfare in California, according to the State Attorney General's office and other reliable agencies. In his campaign of 1966, many of his local leaders and contributors were actively and openly associated with known, right-wing extremist organizations, including the John Birch Society. When frequently challenged to repudiate the John Birch Society—as Nixon had in 1962—Reagan refused. When asked pointedly to comment on why so many Birchers were supporting his candidacy, Reagan replied with boyish logic and a charming smile: "If they support me, that doesn't mean I'm buying their philosophy. It means they're buying mine."

Like many political radicals, Reagan is careless with the facts and, to put it mildly, toys with the truth. There was much press and public speculation—and an apparent loss of credibility—on the way the Governor answered questions about charges that he dropped two staff members who were alleged to be involved in a "homosexual ring." I do *not* join the criticism of Reagan on that issue. It was an awkward and nasty business, and I think it is possible that the Governor, to his credit, was willing to risk some damage to his reputation in an effort to protect the lives and reputations of others. But the obvious examples of Reagans credibility gap are legion.

Sometimes his indifference to facts and the truth was so blatant that he was forced to retract intemperate comments. His charge that an incident at Sonoma State Hospital was "rigged" to make him look bad on the mental health issue was withdrawn later when he admitted, "Perhaps I spoke hastily."

At other times, the truth of Reagan's beliefs varied from audience to audience. In October, 1965, he told a Republican audience in San Francisco, "I favor the Civil Rights Act of 1964 and it must be enforced at bayonet point if necessary." (I'm sure that is the kind of support the Justice Department could do without.) The next year, early in his gubernatorial campaign and before another audience, he said that, if he had been in the Senate, he would have voted *against* the 1964 Civil Rights Bill. Later in the campaign, he corrected himself: "I'll tell you the truth—I don't think really that was a proper thing for me to say."

Some of his quick generalizations are gross distortions of the truth. On May 30, 1965, he said that welfare recipients "are a faceless mass waiting for a handout." On April 12, 1966, he said, "Unemployment insurance is a prepaid vacation for freeloaders." On December 4, 1967, he commented on the state program of medical care for the elderly: "The [Medi-Cal] cardholders never pays a nickel. [The taxpayers] are actually being taxed to provide better medical care for these cardholders than you can afford for yourself." That was untrue, and of course Medi-Cal "cardholders" had been taxpayers all their lives.

In four out-of-state speeches early in his term, Reagan

boasted he had reduced the number of state employees substantially but only by attrition and "without a single firing
or lay-off." The fact was that at that point, 250 employees
had been fired from the Department of Mental Hygiene
alone. In an attempt to prove his argument about the efficiency of private enterprise solving problems, Reagan
boasted, in September 29, 1967, in South Carolina, that his
business allies had provided jobs for 17,500 hard-core unemployed. That figure had been only an early estimate and was
substantially reduced by the business leaders later; at his
December 12 press conference, Reagan admitted he had used
the larger figure while knowing it was not valid.

When he is *opposed* to something, the Governor is even
more irresponsible with the facts. On October 30, 1966, he
said that the Rumford Fair Housing Act was "introduced
into the legislature in the last six minutes of the 1963 session and was forced through hastily and without proper consideration." The truth was that the Rumford bill was introduced early in the session and scrutinized in many
lengthy public hearings. On March 14, 1967, he stated flatly
at a press conference that the people of California had voted
"several times [and] made it unmistakably plain that they
support the death penalty." One resourceful reporter
checked with the Secretary of State to confirm that there had
never been referendum or any other kind of public vote on
the death penalty in California.

Reagan's method of escaping blame for his more extreme
and damaging statements is to denounce the press or question its competence. He was quoted in one speech as saying
that the progressive income tax had been "spawned by Karl
Marx." He denied to reporters that he had made the statement, then perplexed them completely by repeating it in another speech. Some newspapers were paraphrasing when
they repeatedly quoted Reagan as saying, during the Na-

tional Redwoods Park controversy. "If you've seen one tree
you've seen them all." But his actual statement, in a speech
to the Western Wood Products Association in San Francisco
on March 13, 1966, conveyed the same meaning. "A tree's a
tree. . . . How many more do you need to look at?" Reagan
later denied making that statement and, according to Bob
Schmidt of the *Long Beach Independent-Press-Telegram*,
"as much as called the several reporters who so quoted him
liars."

As most political radicals do, Reagan cloaks his extreme
views with a negative sort of nobility. He invokes a few en-
ticing, simple principles to justify his zealous and radical attacks on existing values and systems of government. On October 8, 1969, he won cheers at a Los Angeles meeting of the
National Association of Certified Public Accountants with a
sweeping attack on welfare assistance programs and government spending:

"Either the problems confronting us will be solved by
those who believe in individual freedom—including the
right of each person to spend as much of his own private
wealth as possible—or by those who feel the government
should have claim to more and more of the individual's
earnings. . . .

"What is needed now is an antirevolution—a reformation
of the reformers. Under the false title of liberalism, we have
seen social engineers with calculation and the violence of
centralized power confine, control, and direct the free
rhythms of human life.

"They deny the validity of absolute moral values and reject the spiritual bases upon which that unique being—the
individual person—is founded, and with that rejection, they
destroy the philosophical foundation of our free society."

There is another superficially appealing thrust to Reagan's radical attacks on government: his unwavering and arti-

culate identification with public resentment against taxes. No citizen or society has ever enjoyed paying taxes. With all the affluence of America—and the particular wealth and high per-capita income of Californians—there is deep and strong resistance by the people to taxes. Any Governor, of any party or philosophy, must face up to the eternal fact that the citizens and voters will ultimately resent his pleas for their money. I was aware of the public's basic antitax attitude through my years as Governor, and sometimes worked to modify it. At one point in my second term, I prepared and distributed an article documenting the bargain of services the people were getting for their taxes. It had no effect. The people seem willing to pay their utility bills without an uproar, although the increases for most utility rates have been in excess of tax increases. No matter how eloquent he is, a Governor cannot convince the people to abandon a deep prejudice—and their deepest prejudice is against taxes. The people want the services of government, but they just don't want to pay for them.

Reagan not only rides along with the public's antitax attitude, he accelerates it. His constant antitax and antigovernment pronouncements in recent years have contributed to the so-called taxpayers revolt which is very real in California. The people have turned down innumerable, vital bond issues for public projects. They have also been voting down with frightening regularity local tax increases for schools and other essential services. No politician who wants to survive can go out to wage a general public campaign in favor of the principle and necessity of taxation. But Reagan abdicates leadership and does a disservice to his state and its people by waging war against the whole concept of taxation. He undoubtedly feels fortified politically in his war against taxes when he sees recent public opinion polls that reveal that "taxes, government spending, and inflation" far outrank any other issue (even Vietnam and campus disorders) in the interest and grievances of the people.

The key to everything in government is finance. No matter how obviously worthy a program is, there must be revenue—from taxes—to finance it. There were times during my administrations when, despite my awareness of the public's antitax attitudes, I campaigned hard for a costly program I considered essential—education was the prime example. In 1962, a bond issue to finance university and college construction was defeated by voters in the June primary. Even though I faced the tough fight with Nixon that year, I called the legislature into special session to put the bond issue back on the ballot in November. I campaigned for it, and it won. Often, my administration was able to convince enough of the opinion leaders and the public to be able to boost or improve a service without crippling opposition. A few times, when I considered a program essential and could not drum up widespread support for it, I took a chance and went ahead with it—literally praying that the people would subsequently recognize the merits of my decision. Usually, with time for reasonable consideration, the people accepted the need for a service I had fought for, occasionally alone.

Reagan's handling of state finance has been careless, devious, and contradictory. He has contrived a public reputation as a tight-fisted economizer, while state budgets have soared to record levels during his administration. He developed a public image as a tax-cutter, despite his pushing through the biggest tax increase in history in 1967 (which turned out to be twice as much as necessary). Fiscally, his administration has failed miserably. Behind all the appealing slogans and rhetoric, one fact of Reagan's fiscal failure stands out: State government services have been reduced, while state government costs have increased.

One reason for the failure was the sheer inefficiency and lack of imagination by Reagan's fiscal advisers; another was his stubbornness in opposing some revenue-producing measures. For three years, Reagan adamantly opposed the principle of regular withholding of state income taxes, and clung to the outdated system in which Californians paid their income taxes once a year. I had spent years fighting and arguing for withholding as a modern, efficient, and economical system for collection of income taxes and was close to victory when my second term ended, in early 1967. The press, the people, and the legislature, I am convinced, were ready to accept it. Reagan flatly opposed withholding from his first day in office. Against rising public pressure, he argued the issue on vague psychological grounds: The people ought to be aware of the high taxes they paid, and they would be more aware of it if the taxes "hurt," meaning if they were paid in a large sum only once a year. Through 1967, 1968, and most of 1969, the Governor regularly restated his flat opposition to withholding, sometimes with the statement that "my feet are in concrete" on the issue. In another statement, he said that he could only imagine supporting withholding "if they hold a burning blowtorch to my feet." He even devoted the whole of one of his TV "Reports to the People" to a denunciation of withholding, with such politically paranoic comments as these:

"Withholding is a painless way of extracting your money. And the very fact that it is painless means government is always willing to ask you for more.

"Withholding means you don't watch so closely where your tax money is going because it removes your consciousness of the fact that you are paying.

"But withholding also tends to make the government careless with the management of your money because there is always more where that came from. . . ."

Finally, in the fall of 1969, he succumbed to the overwhelming evidence of the prudence and necessity of a withholding system for state income tax. It is minor consolation that Reagan finally indicated he could learn something new after spending three years as Governor. But the slow learning process and his stubborness cost the state and its people dearly. If withholding hád been established in 1967, the state would not have lost the revenue from taxes of people who moved in or out of the state during each year. Reliable estimates expose the cost of Reagan's fiscal failure and anti-tax stubbornness: California lost $400 million in revenue during the three-year delay in establishment of withholding.

Starting in his 1966 campaign and through three years as Governor, Reagan promised the people that he would provide relief to property-taxpayers and push a general tax reform program through the legislature. He did not deliver on either promise.

Some of the most significant aspects of Reagan's fiscal failure as Governor were summed up by the *Sacramento Bee* in an editorial of February 10, 1970, following the introduction of his 1970–71 budget:

". . . The proposed spending program of $6.48 billion is the highest in history. This undoubtedly is unavoidable because California . . . still is a growing state. The record budget figure is only significant because Reagan is the one who campaigned for office by ridiculing high budgets of previous administrations and promising economy.

"Also important to remember is the Reagan Administration three years ago sponsored the biggest tax increase in history and will need more tax boosts this year to fund the budget and to 'give some money back' to some taxpayers—an attractive program during campaign time. . . .

"The state government's responsibility is to serve the citizens. What is necessary to provide a proper level of service should be placed in the budget. . . .

"[The legislature] has before it several warning signs: Capital outlay for higher education facilities has been sharply curtailed in recent years and the disastrous impact of this may not be felt for several years; the percentage of state assistance to education from the total budget has dwindled from 56 to 50 per cent; there are indications development for public-use facilities at state parks and beaches has slowed considerably; support for agriculture, the state's no. 1 business, has been cut, and many other programs have been eliminated or made ineffective. . . .

"The needs of the people will continue after this year's elections no matter who returns to office."

The deep and continuing needs of the people are one thing; they are not necessarily linked consciously with the immediate, surface *wants* of the people. The public, I sadly discovered in the election of 1966, tends to be bored with reasoned discussion of the issues and to be turned off by challenges about the future. Today's citizen cannot comprehend the fiscal magnitude of a $6 billion budget; he does understand what several hundred dollars of his tax money means. He cannot fathom the growing conflicts of a changing society of 20 million people; he has enough of a problem coping with his teenage son. Government today is not under attack just because of the old suspicions of bureaucracy and political power. Government represents society, and both are so complex the average citizen is intimidated. The complexity—along with the new and unpleasant conflicts seen on television news each evening—turns more and more citizens away from a sense of personal involvement with government. I fear that the people today, thanks in part to Reagan's encouragement, are far more aware that they want to hang onto their tax dollars than they are willing to recognize the need for public services costing billions. I fear that they do want what Reagan offers—to "get the government off our backs." They need to be challenged by leaders who responsibly recognize the complexity of today's whole society. But, in the absence of such leaders and with only the engaging, tele-present personality of Ronald Reagan, they are conditioned to want the reassurances of a simplistic perception of society.

The salient feature of Reagan's radicalism is his simplistic approach to the complex realities of the time. A radical does not like to be encumbered by reason or burdened by doubt. His words and actions must be in sharp focus to make an impact. The radical neither recognizes the possible merits of argument by an adversary nor concerns himself with the difficult process of educating his followers. Reagan, as a political radical, does not seek to provide for the complex *needs* of the people. He gives them what they most consciously *want* now—a simple, pleasant image that reduces the realities of a complex and conflicting society to a low, tranquillizing denominator.

The anxious question that must be asked is: How long can the complex state of California survive as a society when it is dominated by the simple state of Ronald Reagan? There is a lingering momentum from the policies, programs, and attitudes of the progressive political decades in California government. The state endures in some degree of prosperity and peace because of the continuing effects of established programs and policies, which not even Reagan was able to change overnight. But the state grows, the needs of the people increase, the blemishes of injustice spread, the confrontations and conflicts escalate, and the pressures can, within a few years, reach the point of explosion. While they do, Reagan offers little more than a smile and a slogan. He speaks and acts not with a vision of the disaster or opportunities of the future, but rather with both eyes on the simple lens of the television camera.

The danger of the simple, radical politics of Reagan is suggested by Daniel Boorstin in his book *The Image*. Boorstin wrote:

"What ails us most is not what we have done with America but what we have substituted for America. We suffer primarily not from our vices or our weaknesses, but from our illusions. We are haunted, not by reality, but by those images we have put in the place of reality."

12

California and the Future

California is not, as many writers suggest, "the nation in microcosm." Nor is it, as some of the more melodramatic national reporters predict, "the wave of the future." California is a part of and apart from the larger American society. It is both representative and unique. The state's people tend to be creatures of the present; they do not have much of a tradition to dwell in, and they are too busy and active each day to spend much time pondering the future. But, in some subtle way, California does seem to hint at the outlines of our national society of the future. Perhaps the reason for the portentous impression is the rapid pace of social change in California. The future seems to loom up more quickly in the state, the unpredictable happens today, the unexpected may well occur tomorrow.

National reporters who have the job of trying to make

sense of the confusions and conflicts of modern America often come to California for brief visits to seek the answers. Usually, they return to New York or Washington—and their typewriters or microphones—more confused than ever. California, in a real sense, is like an "emerging nation"—and not just in the magnitude of its economy, which is far more viable than most of the emerging nations of Africa and other awakening areas of the world. With its fast and almost revolutionary social change, California suffers as much confusion, conflict, and turmoil as many of the emerging nations of Africa.

To America, those California conflicts seem far more significant because they are closer to home. The changes and turmoil within California today concern and, sometimes, frighten the rest of the nation, as they should. I emphasize again the great diversity of California—a changing society of 20 million people spread over a thousand miles of varying landscape—so I balk again at the task of generalization about the state or of extending the generalizations to the whole nation.

One generalization is both safe and significant: California is not a cohesive community. Particularly between northern and southern California, the split of the California community is deep, and the gap between those two regions of the state is becoming wider as each year passes. It is sad that a state so blessed with natural resources and wealth cannot become a cooperative society with a sense of identity and community; the national implications of the California experience are discouraging. I have reluctantly concluded that California should be divided legally into two states, north and south. The great difference between northern and southern California is not just in physical characteristics and circumstances, creating different problems and needs for the two areas. The deepest difference is in the political attitudes of northern Californians and southern Californians. That political difference is almost as pronounced as between Minnesota and Mississippi.

The movement over the past decade to split California into two states has often been regarded as a joke by outsiders, but it has been taken with utter seriousness by growing numbers of Californians, particularly in the north. State Senator Richard Dolwig's bill to divide the state won majority approval in the State Senate a few years ago. Northern Californians are becoming increasingly apprehensive about political domination by the south, which today contains about 60 per cent of California's population and—after the Court-ordered reapportionment of legislative seats in the mid-1960s—exercises the dominant authority in Sacramento. It is likely that southern California will continue to foist such radical Republicans as Reagan and Rafferty into authority over the wishes of the 40 per cent minority of northern California voters. The political power of southern California has already been exerted many times to the specific detriment of the north. In the spring of 1970, for example, the legislature voted to end a long-standing law that guaranteed northern California at least 45 per cent of highway tax funds for road construction. To fulfill their own need for effective representation in state government and to assure the preservation of their own resources, northern Californians will, in greater numbers, support legal separation of California into two states.

I envision one definite advantage to the establishment of two states of California. With two new states could come complete reorganization of government, the formation of *regional* governments and authority, and the reform of conflicting local jurisdictions—all of which are desperately needed.

Will the legal split of California into two states come? The majority of southern Californians will undoubtedly oppose it for awhile—as they enjoy the new but shaky advantages of political dominance in the state. The ultimate establishment of two states—which would require national as well as California approval—is at least ten years off, but the pressures and movement toward it will grow.

The other portents of the contemporary California scene are more difficult to identify and measure. To gain some understanding of the meaning of California for the future and the nation, however, it may be useful for me to compare the politics of Ronald Reagan—Governor—and Richard Nixon—President. Both men are Californians. Both men fascinate people throughout the nation, Reagan because he is a new and different political face, Nixon because he is in the White House. I claim a unique perspective in comparing these two California politicians. I am the only man who contended with both in election campaigns, just four years apart. My interpretation of the political significance of Nixon and Reagan may offer a few insights about the political and social direction of America.

There are similarities between Nixon and Reagan. Each is a Republican. Each moved up from modest beginnings to prosperity and prominence in the Horatio Alger tradition. Each is a successful product of "packaged politics"—the marketing of candidates by expert political technicians and merchandisers. Each today is skilled in the new and most important medium of communication: television.

There are similarities, too, in the way Nixon and Reagan operate as top public executives. As administrators, the President and the Governor seem to prefer a "team" system and rely on a fairly rigid staff hierarchy instead of probing independently into different levels of the bureaucracy, as John Kennedy did as President and I did as Governor. From their high elective positions, both Nixon and Reagan exercise significant influence in the affairs of their party: both have a strong sense of loyalty and discipline as Republicans, characteristics that most often are lacking in Democratic Presidents and Governors.

Politically, Nixon and Reagan are wary about imposing their will, as individuals, on the long-range issues affecting society. Each is far more inclined to determine and then respond to a pattern of public opinion. Nixon and Reagan easily fall into that category of men who doubt that any individual—or government—can really affect events. Each is more inclined to accept the "free rhythms" of the economy and life.

In specific policies, Nixon and Reagan share similar positions. They favor minimum governmental restriction or regulation of private enterprise. They are actively antagonistic toward welfare programs. They are, at best, lukewarm about using the influence of their offices and voices to achieve racial desegregation. They place lower priority on programs of assistance to the poor than on their efforts to reduce government spending. They cater to and are popular with "states' rights" advocates, particularly in the Southern states (and in southern California, to which many people from the South have moved) and particularly in their antagonistic attitudes toward federal court decisions. Both Nixon and Reagan pay far more respectful political attention to the supporters of Alabama's George Wallace than to supporters of New Left movements.

All of these similarities between Nixon and Reagan are interesting, but not nearly as significant or portentous as their differences.

Reagan, as I have outlined previously, is a radical politician. He represents *extreme* departures from the political traditions and governmental policies of this century, at least. Nixon is not at all radical. He is merely a political conservative, today somewhat reactionary on several basic issues, who respects the "establishment" and existing institutions.

Reagan is profoundly antigovernment. Nixon shares the normal Republican skepticism of centralized authority, but he has been a part of government for many years, recognizes its necessity, and respects many of its functions of service to the people.

Reagan is an antagonist and advocate in the recurring and explosive conflicts of society today. Nixon tries to be—without much success—a conciliator, seeking to mute the passions and mediate the conflicts between people.

Reagan likes to be publicly and verbally involved in the contentious, publicity-attracting struggles of society today. He is not at all reluctant to speak out in strident voice or to move physically and belligerently through the "Politics of Confrontation." Nixon adheres to what he called a "low profile" approach to leadership, speaking out—in measured tones—only when necessary, beseeching the people to lower their voices and passions, and avoiding confrontation with his militant enemies.

Reagan is an impulsive man, personally and politically. He often slips out of the contrived role prescribed by his "packaged politics" technicians to act spontaneously and emotionally. Nixon is cautious, methodical, usually restrained, and has uttered few "shoot-from-the-hip" comments in recent years. One sees him setting down his reasoned thoughts on a neat yellow legal pad in the privacy of his own room.

These are generalizations, and there are exceptions in each category of comparison I have offered. In essence, two significant and basic differences emerge in the patterns of political conduct by Nixon and Reagan.

President Nixon respects and is a part of our system of representative government. Governor Reagan detests that system and seeks to tarnish it in the public mind and tear it down in the state budget.

Second, President Nixon often seeks to use his prominent and influencial voice as a peacemaker, although he does authorize or, at least, tolerate the aggressive adventures of Vice President Spiro Agnew and Attorney General John Mitchell. Governor Reagan is instinctively drawn to the fight; the peacemaking role is foreign to him. He prefers to wage war against one adversary in any important social or political conflict.

One strange similarity in the records of Nixon and Reagan serves to point up the more important differences between the two men today. Reagan today strongly resembles the Richard Nixon of the late 1940's and early 1950's. Twenty years ago, Nixon was a harsh and negative political voice in California and nationally. He stridently and emotionally denounced government, demagogically attacked his political opponents, and regularly castigated whole groups of the population, from Democrats to intellectuals. Under the guise of opposing international and domestic Communism, he was only slightly less ruthless and careless than Senator Joseph McCarthy. As late as the congressional campaigns of 1954, when he toured the country on behalf of Republican candidates while he was Vice President, Nixon was clearly echoing McCarthy charges of "twenty years of treason" against Democrats. The issues in those tragic years tended to be placed in partisan terms more than today and were most often linked to the threat or fear of Communism. In that context, Nixon was an abrasive, contentious, impulsive political figure.

Time—almost twenty years of it—and lengthy service in government and politics mellowed Nixon's voice and modified his extremist positions. It's possible also that he was made a bit more of a tolerant man, a whole man, by the humbling process of two election defeats, for the Presidency in 1960 and the California Governorship in 1962. I hasten to say, for the benefit of the record and the understanding of my Democratic allies, that I do not endorse the positions and policies of Nixon; his mediocre programs and indifferent leadership fall far short of the essential needs and challenges to the nation today. It is only in comparative terms that Nixon has become a politician of moderate temperament.

But, in my opinion, there has been a real change in Nixon in recent years. He is far more careful and seems to have developed a real sense of humor. The impact of the White House unquestionably has a mystical effect upon whoever enters that stately mansion.

At the White House dinner for Earl Warren, the President singled me out by stating, "I see my old friend Pat Brown is here tonight—Pat, I want to thank you for defeating me for Governor, because if I had defeated you I would probably still be Governor, and I really think I can do more good as President of the United States."

While Reagan is often inclined to shoot-from-the-hip statements, Nixon remains almost thoroughly controlled in all his public statements and actions. The President seems to have more dignity.

I really thought that all this meant that Richard Nixon was a changed man, but then came the Carswell matter, and I am today deeply concerned about his objectivity and judgment. As President, he clearly bungled on his nominations of Haynsworth and Carswell for the Supreme Court. Defeated by the Senate, he chose to lash out at that thoughtful, deliberate body for exercising its Constitutional authority to advise and consent on Supreme Court nominations. Even though he waited a full day after the defeat of the Carswell nomination to make a public comment and even though he veiled his anger with a tight smile in front of the cameras, he was reverting to demagoguery when he stated explicitly that the Senate was anti-South. His anger was real, but his purpose was characteristically contrived for its political effect. His statement neatly fit into his "Southern strategy" to solidify his support in that region of the nation. I remain anxious about Nixon as President because of his instinct to become malicious, vindictive, and cynical in moments of defeat or setback. That is the danger of his Presidency. And it conflicts with his very modest claim to a place in the American political tradition.

Ronald Reagan does not fit into that tradition at all. I know that his election as Governor of the biggest state in the nation was no accidental result of momentary public confusion. A majority of Californians—a large majority—liked him, wanted him to be Governor, and voted for him. I am tempted to think—wishfully—that Reagan is an aberration of Californian and American politics, but I suspect that he and the radical political mentality he represents will be with us for many years.

Could Reagan change, as Nixon did, mellowing with time and the influence of the realities of public office? In rare moments of hope, some conscientious observers think he is changing. In his report on Reagan's State of the State address in January, 1970, *Los Angeles Times* reporter Robert Fairbanks wrote:

"The old Ronald Reagan—the Governor of the hard-line, the crackdown, and the simple answer—disappeared Tuesday in a message deliberately aimed at seeking support from California's often fractious youth.

"Unlike his State of the State speeches in 1967, 1968, and 1969, Reagan refrained from attacking that symbol of youthful rebellion, the campus militant. . . .

"Reagan also avoided those simplistic analyses of government problems that were common in his speeches of the past. . . ."

But the hopeful hint of a new, conciliatory, and moderate

Reagan was quickly dashed. Within a few months, he was flailing out in characteristically contentious and simplistic fashion—literally shaking his fists at one group of demonstrating students and later telling the university's Board of Regents that he had "lost all patience" and demanding another "crackdown."

Reagan will not change, I believe, because he is peculiarly removed from what Republican moderates like to call the "mainstream" of politics. Even as Governor, he is strangely removed from government and the Governor's office—and not just because he spends inordinately long periods of time on out-of-state speaking tours. Reagan is fixed and rigid in his attitudes and political temperament and stands above and outside of the compromising, conciliatory, moderate vortex of government that forges conflicts into cooperation. But he is not aloof from the people; he stares earnestly toward them at eye-level, the eye of the television camera, which carries his image regularly into each California home. Reagan is not likely to change, because a majority of the people in those homes, according to most of the polls, favor what they *see* him doing and what they hear him saying. Nothing fortifies or justifies a politician's habits as much as success in the opinion polls.

Even if Reagan were inclined to learn, moderate, and change, there isn't the time. He is not a young man, despite his youthful appearance on television. And there is no time for society. The swift, almost revolutionary changes that are sweeping California—with the tragic outbreaks of violence—will not wait for some slight hope that he might some day become a responsible leader instead of continuing as just another—but powerful—contentious voice.

Could Reagan's influence spread beyond California? Could the simplistic and radical politics of the man become the politics of the nation and of the future? Logically, his personal chances for the Presidency are slim. The incumbent Nixon is likely to have the Republican nomination for the asking in 1972, and, by 1976, even Reagan's boyish good looks will have begun to fade as he celebrates his 65th birthday.

But Reagan remains both a force and a symbol of a new and negative type of politics, which *could* spread outside California and into the future. The pattern of simplistic, antagonistic, radical, and image-dominated politics *could* flash quickly across the nation in the near future as the same social conflicts and complexities that have rocked California flare in the rest of the nation.

As Reagan traveled America in 1968, he spoke often and hopefully about a "prairie fire" of political change roaring across the nation. It was a grisly, but apt, metaphor. The political change of which Reagan spoke and which he hopes would move with the speed of a "prairie fire" means an end to government as we have known it, a revolt of the people against taxes, the elimination of welfare assistance to those "faceless masses" of the poor. A real prairie fire does move with devastating speed, destroying the life of the land. Reagan's political prairie fire could move with greater speed, with the help of television. I believe it would devastate our democracy.

No one can predict the future or project the politics of one state to a bigger region or another time. But I know that many of the ugly social conflicts and threatening political patterns in California today are also occurring in other areas of the nation. Reagan is not the *cause* of social tensions and political radicalism in California now, though I believe that he has aggravated them substantially. The unfortunate political currents evident in California now stem from the confusions, fears, and surface wants of a majority of the people. Reagan is a result, a symbol, and a surface image of those currents. The tides of social tension, frustration, and fear probably run most clearly and swiftly in California, but I know they are running elsewhere in America. The ghetto of Watts in California exploded in the summer of 1965; three summers of racial violence followed in other states throughout the nation. The Black Panthers was organized first in Oakland, California; it, and other ugly racial movements, spread to other cities in America later. The radically right-wing John Birch Society first won substantial funds, members, and attention in such areas of California as Orange County; the Birchers and their armed, violent offspring of the Right later took root in many regions of the nation.

So I have to wonder and worry about the possibility of the simplistic, radical politics of Reagan spreading and disrupting the whole of our national society. I respect my state of California—for its beauties and all the positive contributions of its people to the nation and the world. Thus, I am dismayed that this state, consisting of such great diversity, is now an arena in which democracy itself is threatened. That is the ultimate tragedy represented by the Reagan movement: Democracy, which is based essentially on cooperation between and among diverse viewpoints, is now beleaguered in the most diverse state, California. I respect my country, for the greatness and worth of its democratic traditions and the potential it holds to extend freedom, peace, and justice to all men. Thus I am frightened for the United States that the Reagan "prairie fire" might flash across the country, diminishing democracy and stifling diversity.

Despite the depth of my concern and the harsh judgments of Reagan's political and governmental record in this book, I do not feel personal malice toward him as an individual. He is a man of some sincerity, strong convictions, and presumably good intentions. It has not been my intention to disparage him as a private human being. I just don't believe he belongs in a high, honorable, and powerful public role of leadership, I am depressed by his destructive performance as Governor of California, and I feel genuine fear that he and the movement he represents might come to dominate the nation.

I began this book on a positive note, followed by a lengthy and necessarily negative account and criticism of Reagan's record as Governor. I wish now to end with some positive notes, and a touch of hope after my gloomy and somewhat pessimistic view of Reagan's California.

I have three daughters and a son. My wife and I love them, and, when we hope for the future of California and the nation, we are hoping for the future of the lives of our children and grandchildren. We are also proud of our children, and what they are doing in their lives now.

In October, 1969, I enjoyed a particular moment of pride when one of my daughters told me how she and her husband participated in the antiwar Moratorium march in Los Angeles. I did not agree with all that was said by the speakers at the end of that march, and was disturbed by a few isolated instances of inflammatory talk there. But my daughter and her husband believed deeply in their convictions about the war. They were moved by the experience of joining with thousands of other citizens expressing themselves in a communion of protest and with peaceful steps along the streets of Los Angeles. My daughter and son-in-law even carried their baby with them on the Moratorium march. Reagan, of course, criticized the Moratorium march, and Nixon spokesmen in Washington also disparaged it. But I was touched and pleased that my daughter and her family cared enough to express themselves on a vital issue, and I was moved and encouraged that tens of thousands of individuals like them could still come together from diverse viewpoints and express themselves freely and peacefully in California and America.

Another personal story about one of our children helps to

indicate the element of hope I hold for our society and nation.

In the summer of 1957, when I was State Attorney General and debating with myself whether to run for Governor or Senator, I received a lengthy letter from my son, Edmund, Jr. At that time, he was studying in seminary, but was keenly interested in and perceptive about political events and circumstances in California. He offered me some strong advice and ended the letter this way:

"God has endowed you with certain talents and abilities and has given you opportunities to make use of them. And, just as it is true that you have been given these talents and opportunities, it is equally true that you have been given serious obligations right along with them.

"These obligations consist not only in a just and fair administration of your office, but in making positive efforts to spread and defend the natural law of God. How can the rights of minorities be protected if the entire concept of 'inalienable rights' is being pushed aside by the protagonists of 'situation ethics.' "

I always remembered that advice from my son—through my years as Governor—even though I had resisted his urging in the rest of the letter to run for Senator instead in 1958. I was proud when my son, who later turned to a law practice in California, decided to run for public office in early 1970. He, and many other young men like him, still believe in the worthy opportunity of public service through politics and in government. They have not been overwhelmed or acutely depressed by recent ugly social and political patterns. Instead, they are trying to do something positive, to contribute their energies and talents to restore the health of democracy.

The most dangerous threat to democracy and the nation today, in the final analysis, is not from Reagan and radical politicians like him, nor from the mediocre and indifferent leadership of Nixon. If democracy is undermined and falls, the fault will rest with all those who gave up, who concluded that "all is lost" or "it's too late" and then stopped trying to salvage and strengthen the American political process.

All too many Democrats—in California after Reagan's victory in 1966 and nationally after Nixon's win in 1968—did give up. The polarization of social groups and the increasing recourse to use of force and violence added to the political pessimism. The horrible assassinations of two Kennedys and a King fed the despair. Even many Democratic leaders, some in elective office with the continuing opportunity for influence, pulled back in mute confusion, intimidated by the landslide victory of Reagan and his apparently continuing popularity.

One of the reasons Reagan remained popular was that he was not sufficiently challenged by those many Democrats *and* Republicans who privately opposed his attitudes and actions. For at least a few years in California after Reagan's victory, there was a vicious circle, which reduced Democrats and moderate Republicans to political impotence. The Governor was enjoying a wave of popularity in all areas of the state. His opponents knew that the same voters who had supported Reagan in droves would also be voting for or against them, so, in self-interest, they remained silent on the subject of Reagan. As Reagan continued on through a nightmarishly long political honeymoon without challenge, his popularity solidified and increased. With a few exceptions, moderate politicians and leaders let Reagan undermine our democratic foundations.

The crisis of democracy in California today—and possibly in the nation tomorrow—is not just a partisan threat and challenge. It far transcends the interests and purposes of the Democratic Party as an organization. All of those Democrats and Republicans who believe in representative, Democratic government are obliged to challenge Reagan and try to turn the tide away from radical politics. If not, the simple image of Reagan will continue to soothe the people into indifference on the tough realities of the times; the policies of Reagan will continue to add to the tensions and frustrations of major groups of society; the belligerent public stance of Reagan will continue to foment ever more confrontation, conflict, and violence. Democracy could wither and society could be torn apart by anarchy, if the simplistic, radical politics of Reagan is allowed to persist and spread.

The answer is not for progressive citizens and politicians to engage in petty, carping criticism of Reagan, assuming roles just as negative as, but less powerful than, his. Progressive Californians—and particularly the local and state leaders who want to preserve and strengthen democratic government and politics—must be positive.

First, progressive politicians must appeal to the deeper and more positive attitudes and instincts of the people and voters, not just to their surface confusions and fears, as Reagan does. Any slightly reworded echo of Reagan's negative, simplistic appeal only serves to strengthen him and the radical movement. The people *are* capable of intelligent political challenge and democratic government, *if* they have leaders and candidates who define the challenges and respect the public's basic goodwill and intelligence.

Progressive politicians must develop strong social convictions—and must assert them. All the money, polished television techniques, and campaign professionalism in the state will not usually sell a candidate of negligible or bland beliefs, or one who confines the expression of his deepest convictions to a few hours each Sunday morning. One of the reasons for Reagan's success is that he does have convictions —simplistic and dangerous, to be sure—and he bluntly expresses them. Perhaps as a subtle result of television and

partly because of the increasing disdain by youth for hypocrisy, the public today is more inclined to recognize and
respect sincerity of conviction and to reject political sycophants. Progressive politicians must avoid the old platform
hyperbole and express their deepest convictions plainly and
honestly.

What should be the basic conviction to be asserted forcefully by the progressive politician today, to turn the tide
away from radicalism and anarchy?

One of the pat assertions of frustrated liberals today goes
this way: "Reason, not violence, should prevail."

That's a nice and logical thought, but it doesn't mean
much to the youth, the minorities, the poor, and other
groups of our society who feel betrayed, abandoned, or frustrated by older generations or higher authorities in society's
power structure. The alienated and restless groups within
our society are impatient and angry. They want solid deeds
to match the reasonable words of establishment leaders and
authorities.

The real answer to the politics of confrontation and radicalism should be: Rapid *reform,* not revolution. If society is
not to succumb to increasing waves of conflict, violence, and
disorder, leading ultimately to anarchy and revolution, the
institutions and social practices that produce discontent must
be reformed quickly. Those archaic parts of the power structure that have tolerated or encouraged injustice in our
nation must be changed or repaired soon, or the whole
system of our society and government could be overwhelmed.

The details and specifics of rapid reform would vary. But
the essential conviction that must motivate progressive politicians and dominate their public assertions is a faithful
commitment to *justice.*

Justice, to me, is not an abstraction, and its sponsors are
not confined to courts of law. Social justice is a living,

noble human attitude and condition. It means, simply, that people are fair with one another, individually and collectively. Justice means that men do not repress the rights and lives of other men and that society will not ignore the plight of its members whose lives are darkened by discrimination or poverty.

"Law and order" has been the catch-phrase of the successful politician in recent years. There is no question that laws must govern us and that order should prevail in society. But laws and order will not prevail if they are implemented primarily by belligerence or bayonets. We will not have peace in our land until the injustices of society are rooted out and the institutions and policies that have condoned those injustices are reformed.

Today's progressive politicians face a tough struggle in asserting a commitment to justice and turning the political tides away from the radicalism of Reagan. The struggle will suffer setbacks and will require infinite skill and patience. Democracy itself, in a land as diverse as ours, demands patience from its practitioners. Winston Churchill was right when he said that democracy was a frail and inefficient system —but also the best that man had ever devised. Reagan has lost patience with the inevitable tensions and conflicts of a democratic and diverse society. In March, 1970, he flatly said, in demanding another crackdown on student turmoil, that he had lost all patience with student demonstrations and disorder. The following month, he seemed to welcome a campus "bloodbath." To resist his impatient threat to democratic government, progressive politicians today cannot lose patience in the struggle for a peaceful and just society.

The task on behalf of democracy today is awesome, and I must admit that I am pessimistic about the near future. Social tensions, frustrations, and conflicts mount, and violence is spreading.

My hope—and it is a strong hope—is for the long-range prospects of democratic government and society. And my hope rests with the young. They have a greater sense of justice than any generation in our history, and it is outraged today by the injustices they see still stalking the land. I have confidence in the young, that their sense of justice will endure and that they will not sell it out for suburban materialism and political indolence, as they grow older. As the young learn, work, organize, mature, and vote, they will lead our society away from the precarious path of radicalism and repression. The young, I believe with deep faith, will achieve, for California and America, a truly democratic government committed to human justice.

Index